QUANTUM HUMAN DESIGN™ EVOLUTION GUIDE

2023

USING SOLAR TRANSITS TO DESIGN YOUR YEAR

KAREN CURRY PARKER

HUMANDESIGN
— PRESS —

An Imprint for GracePoint Publishing (www.GracePointPublishing.com)

GracePoint Matrix, LLC
624 S. Cascade Ave., Suite 201
Colorado Springs, CO 80903
www.GracePointMatrix.com
Email: Admin@GracePointMatrix.com
SAN # 991-6032

A Library of Congress Control Number has been requested and is pending.

ISBN: (Paperback) 978-1-955272-73-5
eISBN: 978-1-955272-74-2

Books may be purchased for educational, business, or sales promotional use.
For bulk order requests and price schedule contact:
Orders@GracePointPublishing.com

Other Books and Resources by Karen Curry Parker

Abundance by Design

Human Design Workbook

Inside the Body of God

Introduction to Quantum Human Design™ 2nd Edition

Quantum Human Design™ Activation Cards

*Quantum Human Design™ Activation Cards
Companion Book*

QHD Quantum Activation Card Deck (iPhone App)

Human Design and the Coronavirus

*The Quantum Human: The Evolution of Consciousness and the Solar Plexus Mutation in Human
Design*

Understanding Human Design

Quantum Human Design™ Evolution Guide 2022

Follow Karen and Quantum Human Design on social media

@KarenCurryParker

DEDICATION

To all my students, Quantum Human Design™ Specialists, and Quantum Alignment System™ Practitioners: Thank you for trusting me to be your teacher. Thank you for sharing the gift of Who You Truly Are with the world. I am because you are. I love you!

INTRODUCTION

This book is a weekly guide designed to give you a deliberate way to harness the energy of the Sun and the Moon to support you in creating what you want in your life.

Quantum Human Design is a collection of cross-cultural, ancient, and modern archetypes. An archetype is a pattern of thought or symbolic image that is derived from the past collective experience of humanity.

We experience all of the archetypes in the Human Design chart, either from our own unique charts, our relationships, or through the planetary transits. In other words, we all have all of the chart. We just experience the archetypes of the chart differently depending on the unique configuration of our individual charts.

The colored in or "defined" elements in your Human Design chart tell you which archetypes you carry in your own chart. The "defined" elements in your chart are part of what you must conquer to bring your gifts into the world. These energies represent your soul curriculum, what you're here to learn over the course of your life.

The white or "undefined" elements in your Human Design chart tell you a lot about what you are here to learn from others and from the world. You will experience these archetypes in a variety of different ways depending on who you are with and what energies are transiting in the celestial weather. The undefined elements of your chart represent the themes you are designed to explore through your relationships with others and your interactions with the world.

Over the course of a calendar year, the Sun moves through all 64 of the Human Design Gates. The Human Design Gates contain the energy code for 64 core human archetypes. As the Sun moves through an archetype, it "lights up" that theme for everyone on the planet, creating a theme for the week.

We all deal with the weekly themes. Even if the theme doesn't impact your chart deeply, it will impact the charts of the people around you. The gift of the solar transits is that it gives you an opportunity to work deliberately with all 64 of these core human archetypes and to consciously focus on living the highest expression of these energies in your daily life. The solar transits also bring you creative energies that help you meet the goals you set for yourself each year.

The Moon in Human Design represents the energy of what drives us. In traditional astrology, the new moon phase and the full moon phase represent bookend energies that mark the beginning and the end of a monthly creative cycle.

The new moon helps us set the intention for our goals for the month. The full moon supports us in releasing any energies, beliefs, or blocks that are hindering the completion of our goals.

Lunar and solar eclipses are bookends that mark beginnings and endings. The work we do in between can be powerful, and both internal as well as external. Eclipse energy represents cycles that support you in aligning more deeply with your bigger goals in life and support you in breaking free from habits and patterns that keep you from growing and expanding.

To learn more about the transits and how they affect your personal Human Design chart and your energy click here:

http://www.freehumandesignchart.com

HOW TO USE THIS BOOK

The 2023 Quantum Human Design Evolution Guide is a workbook with a weekly writing assignment, affirmations, and Emotional Freedom Techniques (EFT) setup phrases. If you are not a fan of journaling, feel free to contemplate the prompts in whatever way works for you. You may walk with them, meditate on them, or even discuss them with your friends.

I am excited to share with you updated Quantum Human Design language. Over the years it has become obvious to me the vocabulary in Human Design is in need of an upgrade in response to evolutionary shifts and with respect to new research that shows the language we use is so powerful, it can even change your DNA. I hope you enjoy the new language!

Each of the Human Design Gates has a "challenge" associated with it. This is what you must master to get the most out of the movement of the Sun which occurs approximately every six days. Before you complete the writing assignment, read the challenge for each Gate and contemplate what you need to do to get the most out of each of the weekly archetypes.

This year we've included the Earth transits to help you explore how you need to nurture and ground yourself each week. The energy of the Earth helps you stay aligned and supported so that you can better accomplish the themes highlighted by the Sun. In addition to the solar contemplations, you'll find a short contemplation or exercise to help you stay grounded and nurtured during the week, based on the theme highlighted by the Earth.

The Emotional Freedom Technique is a powerful energy psychology tool that has been scientifically proven to change your emotional, mental, and genetic programming to help you express your highest potential. Each week you may work with a specific EFT setup phrase to help you clear any old energies you may be carrying related to the archetype of the week. (Learn more about how to use EFT here: http://quantumalignmentsystem.com/qas-eft)

You will also find exercises for each new moon, full moon, solar eclipse, and lunar eclipse complete with a writing/contemplation assignment and affirmation. You'll be guided in working with the theme of the lunar cycles and eclipses so that you can make the most of these powerful energies.

Every Human Design year gives us a 365-day creative cycle that supports us in releasing what no longer serves us, and allows us to consciously increase our creative energy, grow, and evolve with the support of the stars.

May you have a prosperous and joyful 2023!

THE THEME OF THE YEAR
2023: The Year of Dreams Coming True, A Sneak Peek into the Future and Reaping the Rewards of Karmic Discipline

The past few years have been tumultuous and full of contrasting and challenging energies. The astrological themes for the past three years have been calling us out to release old patterns of the past and to emerge into a deeper alignment with a personal and collective narrative that creates a larger template for us to build from and expand upon.

We are shedding old stories of powerlessness, limitation and "less than". We are redefining the metrics of our own value, the qualifiers of "success" and exploring how to create more wellbeing, coherence, and collaboration in our lives. We are dismantling all the old structures that bind us to stories that no longer serve us or match our evolved identities.

We are dismantling collective structures that don't uphold our new stories about who we are and, in the gap that's left, we're challenged with beginning the process of building something new— something better...

Many of us are quietly quitting, stepping out of the matrix and exploring the question of what else is possible. We're remembering our creative capacity, reclaiming our true identity and learning to hold a vision for the future that requires us to have to learn to trust in the unfolding of right timing. We are growing our faith muscles and patiently waiting for the path to building a world that is more aligned with abundance, justice, sustainability, and for the true value of all life to reveal itself.

This year the planets bring us a fork in the road. We have a choice to either continue with the old ways and wait for the inevitable crumbling of the foundation or we can take leaps of faith and implement solid, grounded steps that will firmly place us on a new path, expanding upon the dreams of what we truly want and the construction of a peaceful, equitable and abundant world.

For those of you who have done the work and courageously explored all the ways in which you allow yourself to be measured and codified by metrics that don't do you justice, this is a year that will bring you hope—a glimmer of the fulfillment that lies on the horizon

With Saturn transiting in Pisces from March 7, 2023, through February 13, 2026, highlighting Gate 55the Gate of Faith, for most of 2023, we are seeing an opportunity to truly ground our dreams and loftier ideals in practical action. We have the potential to deepen our faith and t discover that building toward a dream that is bigger than we know "how" to construct is not only possible, but actually logical and reasonable.

In other words, we are learning that dreaming and using stories to build a template of possibility isn't ungrounded and lofty. It's in fact an essential part of constructing the world we have been longing for and envisioning for decades.

If we're going to use the exponential power of faith as a key element of growth and movement toward a future that better represents the potential of humanity, we must shed outdated paradigms rooted in old ways of thinking. For those of you who have spent the last few years exiting rooms and spaces that you've outgrown, this year will give you some momentum to start actualizing what you've had the courage to move toward, even when it felt like you were groping around in the dark.

We start our exploration of the Human Design year with a quick look at the Nodes. The Nodes give us the overarching theme of our growth this year, letting us know what work needs to be done in order to fulfill the promise of the years.

Over the course of the year the Nodes transit the 24/44, the 27/28, the 3/50 and the 42/32. These themes continue to remind us to do our karmic work of cleaning past patterns and limitation, to not settle for less than what we want or deserve, making sure that we are living in alignment with our value and values, and that we complete what needs to be finished up and stay the course even when we can't see the materialization of what we're building...yet!

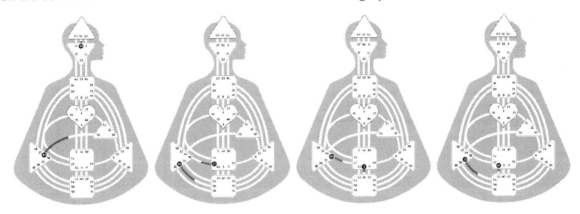

Kiron, the planetoid that reveals our deepest wounds and the path to our gifts, starts the year highlighting Gate 21, the Gate of Self-Regulation, moving to Gate 51, the Gate of Initiation, on March 24. We are learning that the path to remembering our higher purpose is strengthened and emboldened when we cultivate a self-care practice that builds resilience.

Not only do we have to take back control of our stories and who we decide we want to become, we also have to deliberately and carefully construct a practice of internal and external self-generosity. We must nurture ourselves first, both inside and out, in order to create with a clear understanding of who we are and why we are here. When we understand this, we walk with an aura of confidence and with a deep reverence for the unique, vital, and irreplaceable role that only we can play in the Cosmic Plan.

The outer planets, Pluto, Neptune, and Uranus, set the tone and the direction for our collective evolution. These planets remind us of the work that needs to be done, not only for our own growth but for the betterment of humanity.

Uranus highlights Gate 60, the Gate of Conservation, reminding us that progress is best built on what is already working. We are reminded that if we're going to innovate, we need to be mindful of not alienating everyone and tossing everything out. We need to carefully explore what is working and grow it by being grateful for it, no matter how small it may seem.

The temptation with this transit is that we can long to go back to how things were before and we may continue to see a swing back toward outdated ideals. These seemingly backward slides won't last as Pluto reminds us that there is no going back, tempting as it may be. The only way to grow is to shift our focus in the direction we want to be heading. (You can't un-evolve!)

Neptune highlighting Gate 36, the Gate of Exploration, gives us a gentle reminder to hold a vision and sustain it with an aligned frequency of emotional energy and to wait to bring that vision into form only when the timing is right. We are learning to stretch the boundaries and limits of the human story by breaking free from old patterns and creating miracles through emotional alignment and faith. Are you beginning to see the theme here?

Uranus continues its transit through the sign of Taurus until April 2026. We start the year with Uranus highlighting Gate 2, the Gate of Allowing, moving to Gate 23, the Gate of Transmission, on May 9. We've been healing the karma of self-worth and remembering that we are fully supported when we are authentic and honest about who we are. Uranus has been challenging us to explore how much good we are willing to allow in our lives. Do we trust? Are we willing to surrender to the support we deserve?

These questions have been playing out in the arena of our finances in particular. Uranus in Taurus shakes up collective structures that are out of sync with our evolution and growth, dismantling systems that no longer serve higher ideals of sustainability, justice, and equity.

When Uranus moves to Gate 23, we are challenged to trust in our own inner knowing. We have learned that change and transformation are inevitable and that, when we trust ourselves and our own connection to Source, we know what we need to know when we need to know it and we know what we need to do next. The challenge is that not everyone has been doing the same work as you. Gate 23 reminds us to wait to share what we know with the people who truly value our knowing and the wisdom we have, and to not waste our energy trying to convince others who are not ready. This is extremely transformative energy that, when shared with the right people, dramatically transforms what we think is possible.

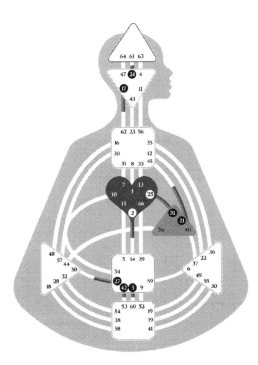

We finish up our overview of the major planetary movements by taking a closer look at Saturn and Jupiter. These two planets "dance" together in the sky, revealing the relationship between the work we must do and the rewards available to us when we do the work.

Jupiter, the planet of blessings and expansion, transits Gates 25, the Gate of Spirit, Gate 17, the Gate of Anticipation, Gate 21, the Gate of Self-Regulation, Gate 51, the Gate of Initiation, Gate 42, the Gate of Conclusion, Gate 3, the Gate of Innovation, Gate 27, the Gate of Accountability and Gate 24, the Gate of Blessings, before she moves retrograde in the fall of the year.

This combination of themes highlighted by Jupiter reminds us that we'll grow and expand when we trust, stay aligned with inspiration and take care of ourselves so that we are strengthened and resilient. When we let go of the old to make room for the new, stay in gratitude, and hold ourselves accountable for doing the inner work necessary to manifest what we want, we expand upon our blessings exponentially. Jupiter reminds us to continually calibrate ourselves so that we are not settling for less than what we truly desire.

Saturn, the great teacher and task master, reminds us that to reap the blessings promised by Jupiter we must keep the faith. Saturn begins the year transiting Gates 49, the Gate of The Catalyst, Gate 30, the Gate of Passion, and Gate 37, the Gate of Peace, until it settles into highlighting Gate 55, the Gate of Faith, for most of the rest of the year.

Saturn reminds us that to create revolutions of growth and expansion in our lives, we must be aligned with our passion, do the work to sustain the vision of what we want to create, and consciously align with whatever routines and habits we need in order to stay peaceful, resource-full, and sustainable. Saturn tasks us with trusting that we are fully provided for and to believe, without a doubt, that the world we dream of is in the process of being formed, even if we can't see evidence of it yet. We must keep the faith.

What does this mean for you?

This is a year that unlocks the momentum that has felt so elusive to you these past few years. To tap into the energy available, you must let go of all stories of limitation and lack that you may have been allowing to block you from building toward what you truly want. Faith, self-care, and consciously crafting an inner and outer environment that supports you in continuing to stay aligned with your purpose and the full expression of your authentic self is essential to staying resilient and being able to pivot during this time of massive change.

Take care of your bodies, your minds, and your spirits so that you stay in a powerful state of receptivity that allows you to know what you need to know and to act on what you need to act on when the time is right.

Not everyone is going to "get" and understand what is happening. Many around you will feel that they are in crisis or chaos. The most powerful and loving gift you can give the world is to keep actualizing your own abundance and potential. Your role this year is to anchor and deepen the foundation upon which you are building an abundant and sustainable life. The more you embody this, the more you can better help and lead others in due time.

It's going to be a great year!

From my Heart to Yours,
Karen

ECLIPSE SEASON

The year 2023 features a series of eclipses upon the Taurus-Scorpio axis, a cycle which started in 2021. This eclipse cycle which will last nearly two years, started with a partial lunar eclipse on **Friday, November 19, 2021**, in 27 degrees Taurus and will end on **Saturday, October 28, 2023**.

Taurus is a reliable earth sign, and Scorpio is an emotional water sign. These eclipses upon this axis will push us to put in the work to make our dreams come true and understand which relationships are worthy of our devotion and which ones we should let go of (remember, if we won't end an unhealthy relationship ourselves, eclipses tend to do it for us).

This eclipse axis is also giving us an invitation to deepen our faith. Taurus rules nature and all things natural. Scorpio is more about the supernatural realm and invokes the depths of faith and the unseen as part of how it moves through the world. Taurus informs us of a crisis in natural resources and nature crying out for a change. Scorpio comes along and promises us a solution to this crisis if we cultivate the faith that we can, and will, create an elegant solution.

This continues to work with the energy of Uranus in Taurus, inviting us to disassemble infrastructures that no longer support the idea that all life is precious and inherently valuable. Continue to expect this eclipse cycle to keep highlighting what needs to come apart before we can begin the process of restructuring.

Eclipses serve as celestial checkpoints. An eclipse is a high-octane celestial event that helps illuminate our karmic path, but just as these cosmic events can be visually striking, eclipses can also be a *bit* dramatic. Astrologically speaking, they speed up time. They open new doors by slamming others shut, so we often find abrupt and sudden shifts occurring during eclipses.

Though the shifts can be jarring, they can help us by speeding up the inevitable.

So, if you've been dragging your feet, an eclipse will be sure to give you that extra push (or shove) needed to take action. While the results can be shocking, remember that these celestial events simply expedite the inevitable—these events were going to happen eventually.

Understanding transits helps you consciously harness the power of the transit and use it to your advantage. This won't necessarily help you avoid the intensity of these catalytic celestial events, but it will help you influence the outcome and better regulate your response to them. Remember, you can't always control what happens in your life, but you always have control over what you do with these events.

During solar eclipses, the Moon is directly between the Earth and Sun, where the Sun and the Moon are said to be in conjunction. For some time, the tiny Moon has the capability to block out the giant Sun and turn off the lights on Earth. This might take away our perspectives in life. Solar eclipses are said to take away fixed patterns and push us into unknown realms. Though this might cause upheavals in our lives, they are excellent growth promoters and powerful catalysts.

Below is a list of all the eclipse dates in this eclipse cycle, including the Human Design Gates high-lighted with each eclipse:

April 20, 2023 - Hybrid Solar Eclipse

Gate 3: The Gate of Innovation

May 5, 2023 - Penumbral Lunar Eclipse

Gate 1: The Gate of Purpose

October 14, 2023 - Annular Solar Eclipse

Gate 32: The Gate of Endurance

October 28, 2023 - Partial Lunar Eclipse

Gate 27: The Gate of Accountability

You will find special eclipse contemplations in the 2023 Evolution Guide inserted on the dates of the 2023 eclipse events.

JANUARY 22, 2023

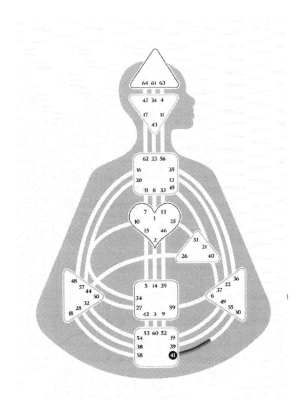

GATE 41: IMAGINATION

CHALLENGE:

To learn to use your imagination as a source of creative inspiration and manifestation. To experience the world and imagine more abundant possibilities. To stay connected to your creative fire.

JOURNAL QUESTIONS:

Do I own my creative power?

How can I deepen the self-honoring of my creative power?

AFFIRMATION:

I am a creative nexus of inspiration for the world. My ideas and imaginings inspire people to think beyond their limitations. My ideas stimulate new possibilities in the world. I am a powerful creator; my creative thoughts, ideas, and inspirations set the stage for miracles and possibilities that will change the story of humanity.

EFT SETUP:

Even though I am afraid my dreams won't come true, I deeply and completely love and accept myself.

EARTH:

Gate 31: Leadership

Explore this week: What is your place of service? Who do you serve? What can you do to feel more empowered and influential in your life?

JANUARY 28, 2023

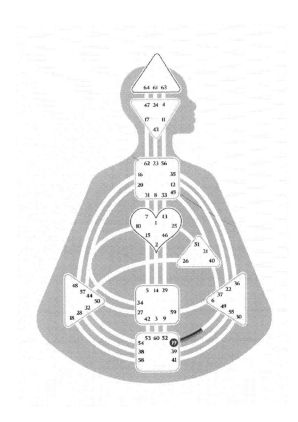

GATE 19: ATTUNEMENT

CHALLENGE:

To learn how to manage being a highly sensitive person and not let your sensitivity cause you to compromise what you want and who you are. To learn to keep your own resources in a sustainable state and in order so that you have more to give. To not martyr yourself to the needs of others. To learn how to become emotionally intimate without being shut down or co-dependent.

JOURNAL QUESTIONS:

Am I emotionally present in my relationships?

Do I need to become more attuned to my own emotional needs and ask for more of what I want and need?

AFFIRMATION:

I am deeply aware of the emotional needs and energy of others. My sensitivity and awareness give me insights that allow me to create intimacy and vulnerability in my relationships. I am aware and attuned to the emotional frequencies around me and I make adjustments to help support a high frequency of emotional alignment. I honor my own emotional needs as the foundation of what I share with others.

EFT SETUP:

Even though it is scary to open my heart, I now choose to create space for deep intimacy and love in my life, and I deeply and completely love and accept myself.

EARTH:

Gate 33: Retelling

What personal narratives are you telling that might be keeping you stuck, feeling like a victim, or feeling unlovable? How can you rewrite these old stories?

FEBRUARY 2, 2023

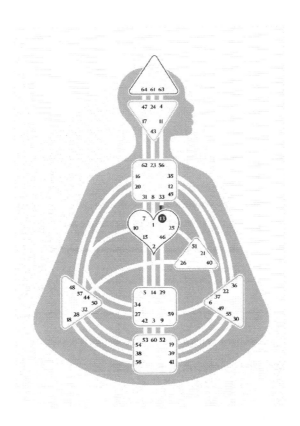

GATE 13: NARRATIVE

CHALLENGE:

To forgive the past and redefine who you are each and every day. To tell a personal narrative that is empowering, self-loving, and reflects your value and your authentic self. To bear witness to the pain and narrative of others and offer them a better story that allows them to expand on their abundance and blessings.

JOURNAL QUESTIONS:

What stories about my life am I holding on to?

Do these stories reflect who I really am and what I want to create in my life?

What or who do I need to forgive in order to liberate myself to tell a new story?

What secrets or stories am I holding for others? Do I need to release them?

Write the true story of who I really am...

AFFIRMATION:

The story that I tell myself and the one I tell the world sets the tone and direction for my life. I am the artist and creator of my story. I have the power to rewrite my story every day. The true story I tell from my heart allows me to serve my *right place* in the Cosmic Plan.

EFT SETUP:

Even though I'm afraid to speak my truth, I now share the truth from my heart, and trust that I am safe, and I deeply and completely love and accept myself.

EARTH:

Gate 7: Collaboration

Make a list of all the times when your influence has positively directed and impacted leadership and important ideas. Stay open to working in teams or groups. Find support and encouragement in collaboration with others this week.

FEBRUARY 5, 2023
FULL MOON

 Leo 16 degrees, 40 minutes

Gate 7: The Gate of Collaboration

Full moon energy invites us to explore what we need to release and let go of in order to stay in alignment with our intentions.

So much of our ability to collaborate and co-create in a healthy, dynamic way is rooted in our lovability and our self-worth. The Nodes this week bring us a theme of not settling for less than what we want, releasing the pain and the patterns of the past and being mindful of not rationalizing staying in situations that do not reflect our value and our lovability.

This full moon invites us to explore how well we work and play with others. Do we serve something bigger than our ego? Can we lead and share without letting our need for recognition get in the way? Are we feeling fully supported, nurtured, and valued? What growth needs to happen for us to be collaborative and supportive creators? How can we better allow ourselves to be supported and nurtured?

 CHALLENGE:

To learn how to manage being a highly sensitive person and not let your sensitivity cause you to compromise what you want and who you are. To learn to keep your own resources in a sustainable state and in order so that you have more to give. To not martyr yourself to the needs of others. To learn how to become emotionally intimate without being shut down or co-dependent.

OPTIMAL EXPRESSION:

The ability to sense the emotional needs of others and your community and know how to bring the emotional energy back into alignment with sufficiency and sustainability. The ability to be emotionally vulnerable and present to increase Heart to Heart connections.

UNBALANCED EXPRESSION:

Being overly sensitive and shutting down or compromising your own needs and wants. Feeling disconnected from others as a way of coping with being overly sensitive. Being emotionally clingy or needy as a way of forcing your natural desire for intimacy.

CONTEMPLATIONS:

How do you manage your sensitivity? What coping mechanisms do you have to keep you emotionally connected in a healthy way?

Are you emotionally present in your relationships? Do you need to become more attuned to your own emotional needs and ask for more of what you want and need?

What emotional patterns do you have that may be causing you to give up what you need and want in order to fulfill other people's emotional needs?

Are you able to be present to the emotional energy around you to help calibrate in a creative, intimate, and sustainable way?

AFFIRMATION:

I am deeply aware of the emotional needs and energy of others. My sensitivity and awareness give me insights that allow me to create intimacy and vulnerability in my relationships. I am aware and attuned to the emotional frequency around me and I make adjustments to help support a high frequency of emotional alignment. I honor my own emotional needs as the foundation of what I share with others.

FEBRUARY 8, 2023

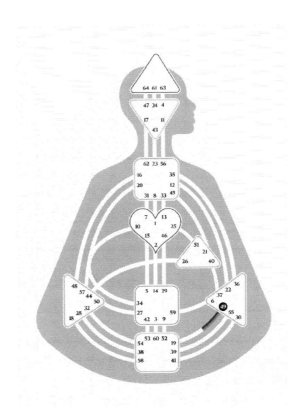

GATE 49: THE CATALYST

CHALLENGE:

To not quit prematurely, failing to start a necessary revolution in your life, to not hold on to unhealthy situations, relationships, or agreements that may compromise your value and worth.

JOURNAL QUESTIONS:

Am I holding on too long? Is there a circumstance and condition that I am allowing because I am afraid of the emotional energy associated with change?

Do I have a habit of quitting too soon? Do I fail to do the work associated with creating genuine intimacy?

What do I need to let go of right now to create room for me to align with higher principles?

AFFIRMATION:

I am a Cosmic Revolutionary. I am aligned with higher principles that support the evolution of humanity. I stand for peace, equity, and sustainability. I align with these principles, and I stand my ground. I do the work to create the intimacy necessary to share my values with others. I value myself and my work enough to only align with relationships that support my vital role.

EFT SETUP:

Even though my emotional response causes me to react or paralyze me, I deeply and completely love and accept myself.

EARTH:

Gate 4: Possibility

Take some time this week to contemplate new ideas and possibilities for your life. Dreaming and day-dreaming support refining focus and alignment this week.

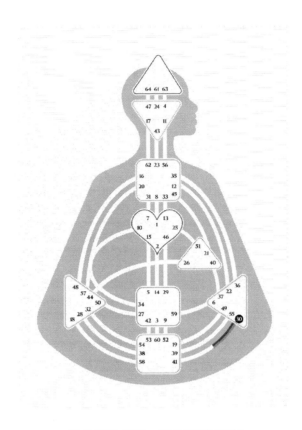

GATE 30: PASSION

CHALLENGE:

To be able to sustain a dream or a vision without burning out. To know which dream to be passionate about. To not let passion overwhelm you and to wait for the right timing to share your passion with the world.

JOURNAL QUESTIONS:

What am I passionate about? Have I lost my passion?

How is my energy? Am I physically burned out? Am I burned out on my idea?

What do I need to do to sustain my vision or dream about what I am inspired to create in my life?

Do I have a dream or vision I am avoiding because I'm afraid it won't come true?

AFFIRMATION:

I am a passionate creator. I use the intensity of my passion to increase my emotional energy and sustain the power of my dream and what I imagine for life. I trust in the Divine flow, and I wait for the right timing and the right circumstances to act on my dream.

EFT SETUP:

Even though my excitement feels like fear, I now choose to go forward with my passion on fire, fully trusting the infinite abundance of the Universe, and I deeply and completely love and accept myself.

EARTH:

Gate 29: Devotion

Who would you be and what would you choose if you gave yourself permission to say "no" more often? What would you like to say "no" to that you are saying "yes" to right now? What obligations do you need to take off your plate right now?

FEBRUARY 19, 2023

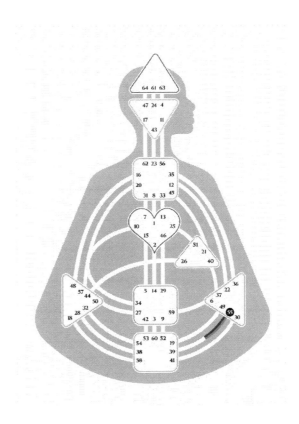

GATE 55: FAITH

CHALLENGE:

To learn to trust Source. To know that you are fully supported. To become proficient in the art of emotional alignment as your most creative power.

JOURNAL QUESTIONS:

Do I trust that I am fully supported? What do I need to do to deepen that trust?

How can I align myself with abundant emotional energy? What practices or shifts do I need to make in my life to live and create in a more aligned way?

Do I surround myself with beauty? How can I deepen my experience of beauty in my life?

What do I have faith in now? What old gods of limitation do I need to stop worshipping?

Go on a miracle hunt. Take stock of everything good that has happened in my life. How much "magic" have I been blessed with?

AFFIRMATION:

I am perfectly and divinely supported. I know that all my needs and desires are being fulfilled. My trust in this support allows me to create beyond the limitation of what others think is possible and my faith shows them the way. I use my emotional energy as the source of my creative power. My frequency of faith lifts others and opens up a greater world of potential and possibility.

EFT SETUP:

Even though I struggle with faith and trusting Source, I deeply and completely love and accept myself.

EARTH:

Gate 59: Sustainability

Notice your energy this week. Are you feeling vital and sustainable? If not, what can you do to rest and renew yourself this week?

FEBRUARY 20, 2023
NEW MOON

 Pisces 1 degree, 21 minutes

Gate 55: The Gate of Faith

New Moon energy invites us to explore how we can deepen our alignment with our intentions and asks us to focus on what we want to grow and expand on in our lives.

Gate 55 reminds us that imagining, envisioning, and trusting that our dreams will come true, even if we don't see any evidence of this in our current reality, is a superpower. We will create in accordance with how much faith we have.

This new moon brings heightened emotional awareness. We are sensitive and deeply attuned to the needs of others. We are learning to create an environment that supports us in "keeping the faith" and we are learning to trust that, when we create with faith, our prayers are inevitably answered.

This new moon also accentuates the theme of relationships and faith in each other. This is a good time to explore what you'd love to be creating in your partnerships and friendships.

 CHALLENGE:

To learn to trust Source. To know that you are fully supported. To master the art of emotional alignment as your most creative power.

OPTIMAL EXPRESSION:

The ability to hold the emotional frequency of energy and the vision for a creation. To trust in sufficiency so deeply that you're able to create without limitation.

UNBALANCED EXPRESSION:

Indecisiveness. Fear and lack. Hoarding, keeping from others, fighting to take more than your share. Not trusting Source and drawing on will to create.

CONTEMPLATIONS:

Do I trust that I am fully supported? What do I need to do to deepen that trust?

How can I align myself with abundant emotional energy? What practices or shifts do I need to make in my life to live and create in a more aligned way?

Do I surround myself with beauty? How can I deepen my experience of beauty in my life?

What do I have faith in now? What old Gods of limitation do I need to stop worshipping?

Go on a miracle hunt. Take stock of everything good that has happened in life. How much "magic" have I been blessed with?

AFFIRMATION:

I am perfectly and divinely supported. I know that all my needs and desires are being fulfilled. My trust in my support allows me to create beyond the limitation of what others think is possible and my faith shows them the way. I use my emotional energy as the source of my creative power. My frequency of faith lifts others up and opens up a greater world of potential and possibility.

FEBRUARY 25, 2023

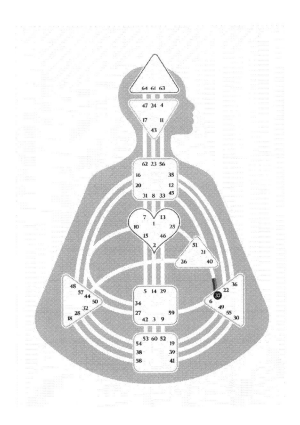

GATE 37: PEACE

CHALLENGE:

To find inner peace as the true source to outer peace. To not let chaos and outer circumstances knock you off your center and disrupt your peace.

JOURNAL QUESTIONS:

What habits, practices and routines do I have that cultivate my inner alignment with sustainable peace?

When I feel that my outer world is chaotic and disrupted, how do I cultivate inner peace?

What do I need to do to cultivate a peaceful emotional frequency?

AFFIRMATION:

I am an agent of peace. My being, aligned with peace, creates an energy of contagious peace around me. I practice holding a peaceful frequency of energy, and I respond to the world with an intention of creating sustainable peace.

EFT SETUP:

Even though I struggle to create peace and harmony in my life, I deeply and completely love and accept myself.

EARTH:

Gate 40: Restoration

We are grounded in rest, renewal, and reconnecting to our purpose this week. Take some time to truly nourish your body, mind, and spirit so that you have a full tank of energy reserves for the days ahead.

MARCH 2, 2023

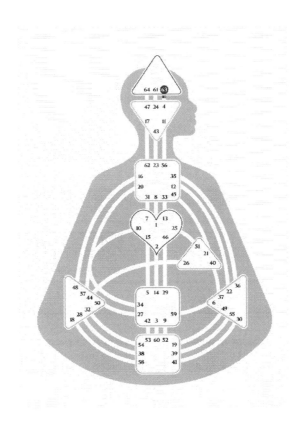

GATE 63: CURIOSITY

CHALLENGE:

To not let self-doubt and suspicion cause you to stop being curious.

JOURNAL QUESTIONS:

Am I curious about life?

Do I regularly allow myself to be curious about what else is possible in the world? In my life?

Do I doubt myself and my ideas?

What needs to happen for me to unlock my need to be right about an idea and to allow myself to dream of possibilities again?

AFFIRMATION:

My curiosity makes me a conduit of possibility thinking. I ask questions that stimulate imaginations. I allow the questions of my mind to seed dreams that stimulate my imagination and the imagination of others. I share my questions as an opening to the fulfillment of potential in the world.

EFT SETUP:

Even though I struggle with trusting myself, I now choose to relax and know that I know. I listen to my intuition. I abandon logic and let my Higher Knowing anchor my spirit in trust, and I deeply and completely love and accept myself.

EARTH:

Gate 64: Divine Transference

How can you embrace your dreams and stop judging them even if you don't know how to yet?

MARCH 7, 2023
FULL MOON

Virgo 16 degrees, 40 minutes

Gate 64: The Gate of Divine Transference

Full moon energy invites us to explore what we need to release and let go of in order to stay in alignment with our intentions.

This full moon invites us to explore our inner and outer environment and to gauge whether our environment is supporting our creativity, imagination, and connection to Source. The light of this moon promises to inspire us, to give us a "big picture" view of what else is possible for us.

We are invited to explore new ways to construct our life and our world to enhance our inner peace, to become more receptive and to become vessels of inspiration. We're also encouraged to release any doubts or limiting beliefs that hold us back from trusting that our dreams can become our reality.

CHALLENGE:

To not let the power of your big ideas overwhelm you and shut down your dreaming and creating. To get lost in the pressure of answering the question "how?"

OPTIMAL EXPRESSION:

The ability to receive a big idea and to serve the idea by giving it your imagination and dreaming. To trust that you'll know how to implement the idea if it is yours to make manifest. To hold the energy of an idea for the world.

UNBALANCED EXPRESSION:

To feel pressure to try to "manifest" a big idea. To feel desperate, inadequate or un-grounded if you don't know how to make an idea a reality. To feel deep mental pressure to figure out an idea. To give up dreaming.

CONTEMPLATIONS:

What do I do to take care of my big ideas?

How do I feel about having dream but not always solutions?

How can I stop judging the gift of my dreams?

Do I trust that the "how" of my ideas will be revealed? How can I deepen this trust?

AFFIRMATION:

I am a conduit for expansive thinking. My inspirations and ideas create the seeds of possibility in my mind and in the mind of others. I honor the dreams that pass through my mind and allow my big ideas to stimulate my imagination and the imagination of others. I trust the Universe to reveal the details of my dreams when the time is right. I use the power of my dreams to stimulate a world of possibility and expansion.

MARCH 8, 2023

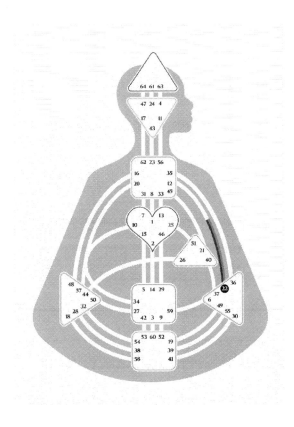

GATE 22: SURRENDER

CHALLENGE:

To trust that your passions and deepest desires are supported by the Universal flow of abundance. To have the courage to follow your passion and know that you will be supported. To learn to regulate your emotional energy so that you have faith that everything will unfold perfectly.

JOURNAL QUESTIONS:

Where am I denying my passion in my life? Where have I settled for less than what I want because I'm afraid I can't get what I want?

What do I need to do to fully activate my passion? What is one bold step toward my genius that I could take right now?

Do I trust the Universe? What do I need to do to deepen my trust?

Do I have a regular practice that supports me in sustaining a high frequency of emotional energy and alignment?

What needs to be healed, released, aligned, and brought to my awareness for me to deepen my faith?

AFFIRMATION:

I am a global change agent. I am inspired with passions that serve the purpose of transforming the world. I trust that my emotions and my passion will align me with faith and the flow of resources I need to fulfill my Life Purpose. When I let go and follow my passion, I am given everything I need to change the world.

EFT SETUP:

Even though it is hard to trust in my support, I now choose to trust anyway, and I deeply and completely love and accept myself.

EARTH:

Gate 47: Mindset

How can you cultivate more hope and optimism? This week practice enjoying all of your ideas for the sake of enjoying them without the expectation that you need to figure out how to turn those ideas into reality.

MARCH 13, 2023

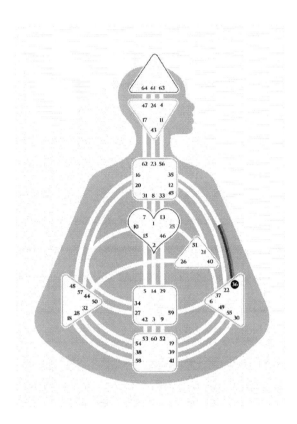

GATE 36: EXPLORATION

CHALLENGE:

To not let boredom cause you to leap into chaos. To learn to stick with something long enough to become skillful and to bear the fruits of your experience.

JOURNAL QUESTIONS:

How does boredom impact my life? What do I do when I feel bored? What can I do to keep myself aligned even when I'm bored?

What stories have I experienced that have shattered old patterns and expectations? How have my stories changed or inspired others?

What do I do to maintain or sustain emotional alignment? What do I need to add to my daily practice to amp up my emotional energy around my intentions?

AFFIRMATION:

My experiences and stories break old patterns and push the boundaries of what is possible for humanity. I defy patterns and I create miracles through my emotional alignment with possibility. I hold my vision and maintain my emotional energy as I wait to bear the fruit of my intentions and my visions.

EFT SETUP:

Even though it is scary to be out of my comfort zone, I now choose to push myself into something new and more aligned with my Truth, and I deeply and completely love and accept myself.

EARTH:

Gate 6: Impact

Contemplate how you feel about abundance. List all the different ways you have been abundantly supported in the past.

MARCH 19, 2023

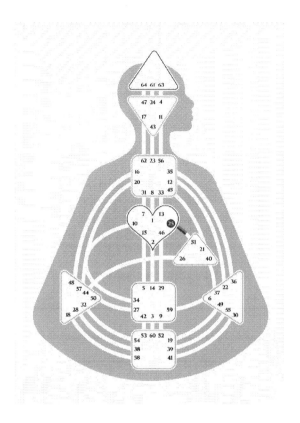

GATE 25: SPIRIT

CHALLENGE:

To trust the Divine Order in all of your life. To learn to connect with Source as the path to creating wellbeing in your life. To remember that your life serves an irreplaceable role in the Cosmic Plan and to honor that role and to live from it. To trust Source.

JOURNAL QUESTIONS:

Do I trust Source?

Do I have a regular practice that connects me to Source?

Do I know my Life Purpose?

Am I living true to my Purpose?

How can I deepen my connection to my Purpose?

AFFIRMATION:

I am an agent of the Divine. My life is the fulfillment of Divine Order and the Cosmic Plan. When I am connected to Source, I serve my right place. I take up no more than my space and no less than my place in the world. I serve, and through serving I am supported.

EFT SETUP:

Even though in the past, I was afraid to follow my heart, I now choose to do what is right for me and know that I am fully supported, and I deeply and completely love and accept myself.

EARTH:

Gate 46: Embodiment

What do you need to do to better love and nurture your body? This week spend some time in front of the mirror and ask your body what it needs to embody greater vitality.

MARCH 21, 2023
NEW MOON

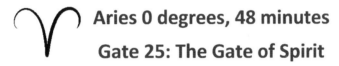 **Aries 0 degrees, 48 minutes**

Gate 25: The Gate of Spirit

New Moon energy invites us to explore how we can deepen our alignment with our intentions and asks us to focus on what we want to grow and expand on in our lives.

The Moon has been moving us along a powerful path of evolution and growth. The themes of this year's lunar placements so far have given us a deep invitation to explore our relationship with Source/God/Universe or whatever word feels comfortable to you.

With Saturn highlighting Gate 55, we are students in the school of faith. We trust that, even if things look grim, our inner vision will be translated to the outer world if we keep the faith. The Moon is deepening this lesson for us.

This new moon offers an invitation to explore and rekindle our relationship with Source, to commit more deeply to our higher purpose and to explore how we can deepen our faith.

Spend some time with this new moon and ask how you can deepen our connection to the Divine and to better take your right place in the Cosmic Plan—that place that only YOU can fulfill.

CHALLENGE:

To trust the Divine Order in all aspects of your life. To learn to connect with Source as the path to creating wellbeing in your life. To remember that your life serves an irreplaceable role in the Cosmic Plan and to honor that role and live from it. To trust Source.

OPTIMAL EXPRESSION:

To connect with Source with consistency and diligence as to fulfill your Divine Purpose and the true story of Who You Are and the role you play in the Cosmic Plan. To use your alignment with Source as a way of healing the world.

UNBALANCED EXPRESSION:

Fear and mistrust of Spirit. Using your life strictly for personal gain, regardless of the impact on others. Ego in the lowest expression. Not feeling worthy of being loved by Source and using your willpower to create instead of your alignment.

CONTEMPLATIONS:

Do I trust Source?

Do I have a regular practice that connects me to Source?

Do I know my Life Purpose? Am I living true to my Purpose? How can I deepen my connection to my Purpose?

AFFIRMATION:

I am an agent of the Divine. My life is the fulfillment of Divine Order and the Cosmic Plan. When I am connected to Source, I serve my right place. I take up no more than my space and no less than my place in the world. I serve, and through serving, I am supported.

MARCH 25, 2023

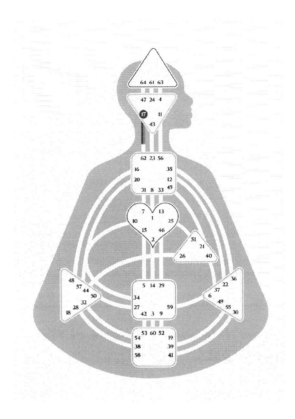

GATE 17: ANTICIPATION

CHALLENGE:

To learn to share your thoughts about possibilities only when people ask for them. To not let doubt and suspicion keep you from seeing the potential of positive outcomes.

JOURNAL QUESTIONS:

What do I need to do to manage my insights and ideas so that they increase the options and potential of others?

How do I feel about holding back from sharing my insights until the timing is right?

What can I do to manage my need to share without waiting for the right timing?

What routines and strategies do I need to cultivate to keep my perspectives expanding and possibility-oriented?

How can I improve my ability to manage doubt and fear?

AFFIRMATION:

I use the power of my mind to explore possibilities and potential. I know that the inspirations and insights I have created exploration and experimentation that can inspire the elegant solutions necessary to skillfully control the challenges facing humanity.

EFT SETUP:

Even though I have a lot of ideas and thoughts to share, I trust that the insights I have to offer are too important to blurt out and I wait for the right people to ask. I deeply and completely love and accept myself.

EARTH:

Gate 18: Re-Alignment

This week explore where you need to add more joy to your life. Do you have any old stories you need to release around the need to be right?

MARCH 30, 2023

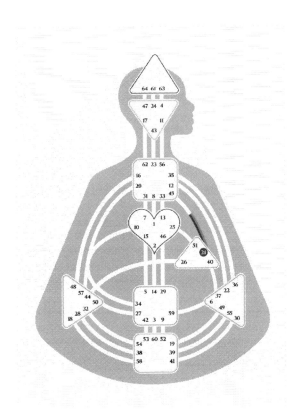

GATE 21: SELF-REGULATION

CHALLENGE:

To learn to let go. To become proficient at self-regulation. To release the need to control others and circumstances. To trust in the Divine and to know that you are supported. Knowing that you are worthy of support, and you don't have to overcompensate.

JOURNAL QUESTIONS:

Where do I need to release control in my life?

Do I trust the Universe?

Do I value myself? Do I trust that I will be supported in accordance with my value?

What do I need to do to create an internal and external environment of self- generosity?

What needs to be healed, released, aligned, and brought to my awareness for me to embrace my true value?

AFFIRMATION:

I am worthy of claiming, protecting, and defending my rightful place in the world. I create an inner and outer environment that is self-generous, and I regulate my environment to sustain a high frequency of alignment with my true value. I know that I am an irreplaceable and precious part of the Cosmic Plan and I create my life to reflect the importance of my right place in the world.

EFT SETUP:

Even though in the past I felt like I had to control everything, I now surrender to Source and know that TRUE abundance, is available to me when I let go and let the Universe do the work, and I deeply and completely love and accept myself.

EARTH:

Gate 48: Wisdom

Make a list of all of your trainings, all of the skills you have and all of the knowledge you've gleaned from your life experiences. Take some time to truly acknowledge what you know.

APRIL 5, 2023

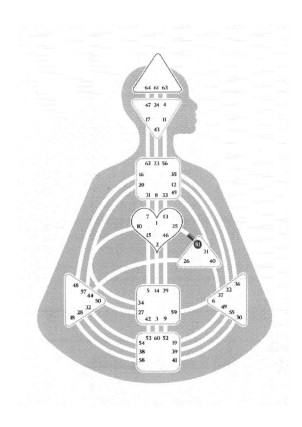

GATE 51: INITIATION

CHALLENGE:

To not let the unexpected cause you to lose your faith. To not let a pattern of unexpected events cause you to lose your connection with your purpose and Source. To learn to use the power of your own story of initiation to initiate others into fulfilling their rightful place in the Cosmic Plan.

JOURNAL QUESTIONS:

What have shock and the unexpected taught me in my life?

How can I deepen my connection to Source?

How can my experiences of initiation be shared with others? What am I here to wake people up to?

AFFIRMATION:

I navigate change and transformation with grace. I know that when my life takes a twist or a turn, it is my soul calling me out to serve at a higher level. I use disruption as a catalyst for my own growth and expansion. I am a teacher and an initiator. I use my ability to transform pain into growth and power to help others navigate through crisis and emerge on the other side of crisis empowered and aligned.

EFT SETUP:

Even though things are not turning out as I expected, I now choose to embrace the unexpected and trust that the Universe is always serving my Greater Good, and I deeply and completely love and accept myself.

EARTH:

Gate 57: Instinct

Notice your intuition this week. What does your intuition feel like to you? Sometimes doing a retrospective analysis of your intuition and instinct makes it clear how your intuitive signals work.

APRIL 5, 2023
FULL MOON

 Libra 16 degrees, 7 minutes

Gate 57: The Gate of Instinct

Full moon energy invites us to explore what we need to release and let go of in order to stay in alignment with our intentions.

In order to be more deeply dialed into our purpose and our faith, we must have a clear connection to our Inner Wisdom—the whisperings of intuition that guide us into fulfilling the next right steps ahead of us in our creative process. This full moon is an invitation to explore your self-trust and your connection to your Inner Wisdom.

The most common block to trusting your intuition is doubt. This full moon invites you to suspend doubt and remember the power of your intuition. How does Inner Wisdom and "knowingness" feel inside your body? How does it sound? What do you need to heal, release, align or clear to deepen the trust in your intuition?

 ## CHALLENGE:

To learn to trust your own insights and gut. To learn to tell the difference between an instinctive response versus a fear of the future. To master your connection to your sense of "right" timing.

OPTIMAL EXPRESSION:

The ability to sense when it is the right time to act. To intuitively know what needs to be made ready to be prepared for the future and to follow through on it.

UNBALANCED EXPRESSION:

To be so afraid of the future that you are paralyzed. To not trust yourself and your own instinct. To know what needs to be done to prepare for the future and to fail to act on it.

CONTEMPLATIONS:

Do I trust my intuition? What does my intuition feel like to me?

Sometimes doing a retrospective analysis of intuition and instinct makes it more clear how the intuitive signal works. What experiences in the past have I had that I "knew" I should or shouldn't do? How have I experienced my intuition in the past?

When I think about moving forward in my life, do I feel afraid? What am I afraid of? What can I do to mitigate the fear?

What impulses am I experiencing that are telling me to prepare for what's next in my life? Am I acting on my impulses? Why or why not?

AFFIRMATION:

My Inner Wisdom is deeply connected to the pulse of Divine Timing. I listen to my Inner Wisdom and follow my instinct. I know when and how to prepare for the future. I take guided action and I trust myself and Source.

APRIL 11, 2023

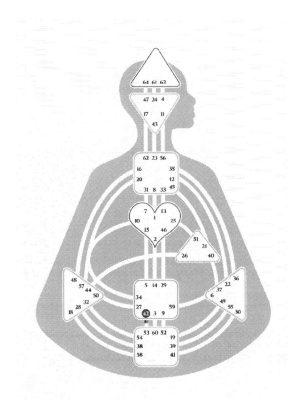

GATE 42: CONCLUSION

CHALLENGE:

To learn to bring things to completion. To allow yourself to be led to where you need to be to finish things. To value your ability to know how to finish and to learn to give up your need to try to start everything. To finish things in order to create space for something new.

JOURNAL QUESTIONS:

Do I own and value my natural gift of knowing how to bring things to completion?

What things in my life do I need to finish in order to make room for something new?

Am I holding on to old circumstances and patterns because I'm afraid to let them go?

Do I judge myself for not starting things? How can I learn to be gentler with myself?

AFFIRMATION:

I am gifted at knowing when and how to finish things. I respond to bringing events, experiences, and relationships to a conclusion in order to create space for something new and more abundant. I can untangle the Cosmic entanglements that keep people stuck in old patterns. My ability to re-align and complete things helps others create space for transformation and expansion.

EFT SETUP:

Even though I have hesitated in the past to finish what I needed to finish in order to make room for something new and better, I now choose to bring things to a powerful ending. I know that I am taking strong action to create space for what I truly want to create in my life, and I deeply and completely love myself.

EARTH:

Gate 32: Endurance

What actionable steps do you need to complete to be ready for creating what you want? Do one thing to lay the foundation for your dreams this week.

APRIL 17, 2023

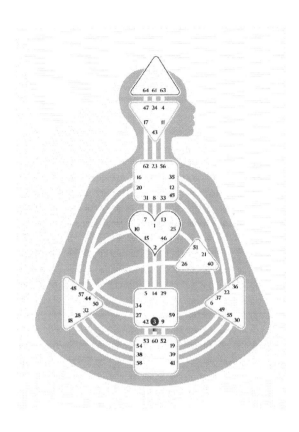

GATE 3: INNOVATION

CHALLENGE:

To learn to trust in Divine Timing and to know that your ideas and insights will be transmitted to the world when the world is ready.

JOURNAL QUESTIONS:

Where has Divine Timing worked out in my life? What has waiting taught me?

Do I trust Divine Timing?

If the opportunity to share my ideas with the world presented itself today, would I be ready? If not, what do I need to prepare to be ready?

AFFIRMATION:

I am here to bring change to the world. My natural ability to see what else is possible in order to create something new is my strength and my gift. I patiently cultivate my inspiration and use my understanding of what is needed to help evolve the world.

EFT SETUP:

Even though it is scary to take the first step, I now trust the Universe and my ability to be innovative and know that I stand on the cusp of the fulfillment of my *big dreams*. I deeply and completely love and accept myself.

EARTH:

Gate 50: Nurturing

This week practice taking care of yourself first—without guilt—so that you can better take care of others!

APRIL 19, 2023
NEW MOON/HYBRID SOLAR ECLIPSE

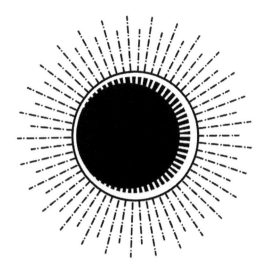

 Aries 29 degrees, 49 minutes/ Aries 29 degrees, 52 minutes
Gate 3: The Gate of Innovation

New Moon energy invites us to explore how we can deepen our alignment with our intentions and asks us to focus on what we want to grow and expand on in our lives.

Eclipse energy amplifies the intensity of the new moon.

A hybrid solar eclipse is a rare type of eclipse. It occurs as the Moon passes between the Earth and the Sun. From some places, it is visible as an annular eclipse. Meanwhile, from other areas, it is visible as a total eclipse. The next hybrid eclipse is predicted to occur on November 14, 2031.

A solar eclipse signifies new beginnings. Not only this, but the solar eclipse exposes all that is hidden and not visible. The eclipse also marks an end to what has already ended. Thus, during this eclipse, many of you who did not get closure from events of the past will eventually find total closure.

As this hybrid solar eclipse occurs in Aries, you will get a lot of energy to start new things or carry on your affairs with great intention, focus and courage. In addition, this eclipse will bring out your creativity. You will be persistent in your pursuits and won't take no for an answer.

The energy of this eclipse and new moon is one of new beginnings. The old stories have fallen away. The past is done. We must reap the blessings from our experiences of the past and move forward in a future that we create, and we choose.

CHALLENGE:

To learn to trust in Divine Timing and to know that your ideas and insights will be transmitted to the world when the world is ready.

OPTIMAL EXPRESSION:

The ability to embrace and integrate new ideas and new ways of doing things. To learn to stay in appreciation for your unique way of thinking and being and to trust that, as an innovator on the leading edge of consciousness, your time to transmit what you're here to bring forth will come, so you wait and cultivate your ideas with patience.

UNBALANCED EXPRESSION:

To feel pressured and panicked about the need to share an idea or innovation. To burn yourself out trying to override Divine Timing.

CONTEMPLATIONS:

Where has Divine Timing worked out in my life? What has waiting taught me?

Do I trust Divine Timing?

AFFIRMATION:

I am here to bring change to the world. My natural ability to see what else is possible in order to create something new is my strength and my gift. I patiently cultivate my inspiration and use my understanding of what is needed to help evolve the world.

APRIL 22, 2023

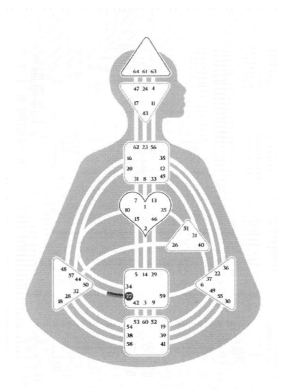

GATE 27: ACCOUNTABILITY

CHALLENGE:

To care without over-caring. To allow others to assume responsibility for their own challenges and choices. To learn to accept other people's values. To not let guilt cause you to compromise what is good and right for you.

JOURNAL QUESTIONS:

Am I taking responsibility for things that aren't mine to be responsible for? Whose problem is it? Can I return the responsibility for the problem back to its rightful owner?

What role does guilt play in motivating me? Can I let go of the guilt? What different choices might I make if I didn't feel guilty?

What obligations do I need to set down for me to take better care of myself?

Are there places where I need to soften my judgments of other people's values?

AFFIRMATION:

I have a nurturing and loving nature. It is my gift to be able to love and care for others. I know that the greatest expression of my love is to treat others as capable and powerful. I support when necessary, and I let go with love so my loved ones can discover their own strength and power.

EFT SETUP:

Even though it is hard to say no, I now choose to take the actions that are correct for me. I release my guilt, and I deeply and completely love and accept myself.

EARTH:

Gate 28: Adventure/Challenge

Where do you need to cultivate a sense of adventure in your life? Do one adventurous thing this week!

APRIL 28, 2023

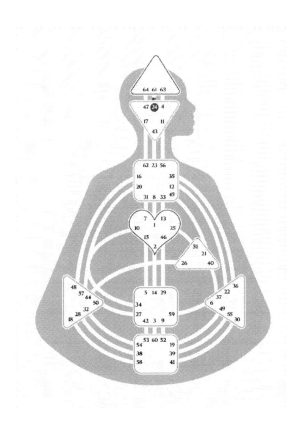

GATE 24: BLESSINGS

CHALLENGE:

To learn to allow what you truly deserve in your life. To not rationalize an experience that allowed for less than you deserve. To find the blessings and power from painful experiences and to use them as catalysts for transformation.

JOURNAL QUESTIONS:

What are the blessings I learned from my greatest painful experiences? Can I see how these experiences served to teach me? What did I learn?

What am I grateful for from the past?

Where might I be rationalizing staying stuck or settling for less than what I really want or deserve? What do I need to do to break out of this pattern?

AFFIRMATION:

I embrace the Mystery of Life with the awareness that the infinite generosity of the Universe gives me blessings in every event in my life. I find the blessings from the pain. I grow and expand beyond the limitations of my experiences and stories. I use what I have learned to create a life and circumstances that reflect the miracle that I am.

EFT SETUP:

Even though it is scary to start something new... I am afraid I am not ready... I now choose to courageously embrace the new and trust that everything is in Divine Order, and I deeply and completely love and accept myself.

EARTH:

Gate 44: Truth

What patterns from the past are holding you back from allowing yourself to see and embody your true worth? What old patterns do you need to release this week?

MAY 4, 2023

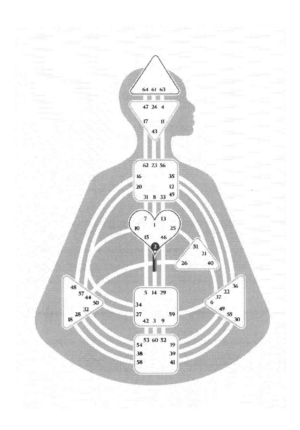

GATE 2: ALLOWING

CHALLENGE:

To love yourself enough to open to the flow of support, love, and abundance. To incrementally increase over the course of your life what you're willing to allow yourself to receive. To learn and appreciate that you are valuable and lovable simply because you exist.

JOURNAL QUESTIONS:

Do I ask for help when I need it? Why or why not?

Do I trust the Universe/God/Spirit/Source to support me in fulfilling my intentions?

Am I grateful for what I have? Make a list of everything I'm grateful for.

Can I transform my worry into trust?

Do I believe that I deserve to be supported?

AFFIRMATION:

I allow myself to receive the full flow of resources and abundance I need to fully express all of who I am. I recognize that my life is a vital, irreplaceable part of the Cosmic tapestry and I receive all that I need because it helps me contribute all that I am.

EFT SETUP:

Even though I am scared because nothing looks like I thought it would, I now choose to relax, trust, and receive the support that I am designed to receive. I know that I will be supported in expressing my true self, and I deeply and completely love and accept myself.

EARTH:

Gate 1: Purpose

Spend time this week thinking about your Purpose and the gifts you long to give the world. How aligned are you with your Purpose?

MAY 5, 2023
FULL MOON/PENUMBRAL LUNAR ECLIPSE

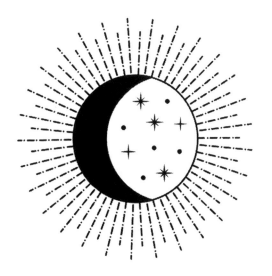

♏ Scorpio, 14 degrees, 57 minutes/Scorpio, 14 degrees, 52 minutes
Gate 1: The Gate of Purpose

Full moon energy invites us to explore what we need to release and let go of in order to stay in alignment with our intentions. Eclipse energy amplifies the intensity of the full moon.

The energy of Gate 1, the Gate of Purpose, is complex and powerful. Gate 1 reminds us that we are each unique, vital, and irreplaceable parts of the Cosmic Plan and that fulfilling the relentlessly authentic expression of who we were born to be is key to not only creating a great life for yourself, but also evolving the world. Your life and the story of Who You Are matters—a lot!

Fully claiming and expressing our authentic self requires that we clear any old stories, beliefs and conditioning around our value and self-worth. When we release any old ideas, stories and experiences that have denied our value, not only do we clear the path for authentic self-expression, but we also position ourselves to receive all the support we need to be who we are in the world. This is the essential contemplation that this full moon and eclipse brings us.

Use the power of this full moon eclipse to explore what you need to release, heal, or align in order to feel safe and powerful when expressing your truth. What needs to change so that you can BE relentlessly and unapologetically authentic?

You being YOU is your Life Purpose.

CHALLENGE:

To discover a personal, meaningful, and world-changing narrative that aligns with a sense of purpose and mission. "I am..." To learn to love yourself enough to honor the idea that your life is the canvas and you are the artist. What you create with your life IS the contribution you give the world.

OPTIMAL EXPRESSION:

The ability to know the Authentic Self and a deep connection with a Life Purpose.

UNBALANCED EXPRESSION:

An erratic or purposeless life, panic, and a feeling of failing at a life mission, pressure to create something unique in the world, struggle to find purpose, hiding because the purpose feels too big, too much or egotistical.

CONTEMPLATIONS:

Am I fully expressing my authentic self?

What needs to be healed, released, aligned, or brought to my awareness for me to more deeply express my authentic self?

Where am I already expressing who I am?

Where have I settled or compromised? What needs to change?

Do I feel connected to my Life Purpose? What do I need to do to deepen that connection?

AFFIRMATION:

My life is an integral part of the cosmos and the Divine Plan. I honor my life and know that being the full expression of who I am is the purpose of my life. The more I am who I am, the more I create a frequency of energy that supports others in doing the same. I commit to exploring all of who I am.

MAY 10, 2023

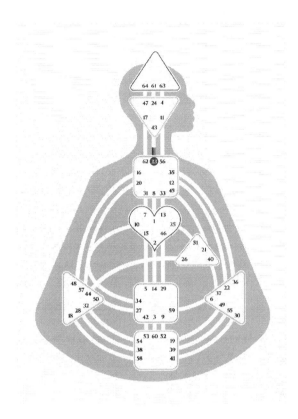

GATE 23: TRANSMISSION

CHALLENGE:

To recognize that change and transformation are inevitable. To know what needs to happen next, to wait for the right timing and the right people to share your insights with. To not jump the gun and try to convince people to understand what you know. To not let yourself slip into negativity and despair when people aren't ready.

JOURNAL QUESTIONS:

How can I strengthen my connection to Source?

Do I trust what I know? What comes up for me when I know something, but I don't know how I know what I know?

How do I handle myself when I know something, but the people around me aren't ready to hear it yet?

AFFIRMATION:

I change the world with what I know. My insights and awarenesses have the ability to transform the way people think and perceive the world. I know that my words are powerful and transformative. I trust that the people who are ready for the change that I bring will ask me for what I know. I am a vessel for my knowingness, and I nurture myself while I wait to share what I know.

EFT SETUP:

Even though in the past I shut down my voice, I now speak my truth and offer the contribution of my unique spirit to the world, and I deeply and completely love and accept myself.

EARTH:

Gate 43: Insight

This week you're learning to trust your "knowingness." Practice trusting your inner knowing and the thoughts and ideas you have. Watch for self-doubt and don't discount what you know even if you don't know how you know what you know.

MAY 16, 2023

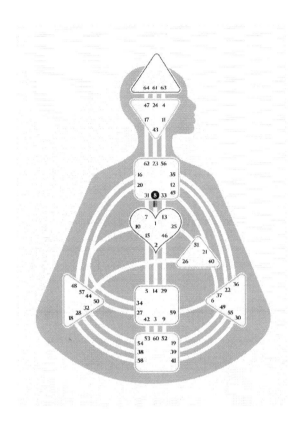

GATE 8: FULFILLMENT

CHALLENGE:

To learn to express yourself authentically. To wait for the right people to see the value of who you are and to share yourself with them, with vulnerability and through all of your heart. To learn to trust that you are a unique expression of the Divine with a purpose and a path. To find that path and to walk it without self-judgment or holding back.

JOURNAL QUESTIONS:

Do I feel safe being vulnerable?

What experiences have caused me to feel unsafe expressing my true self? Can I re-write those stories?

What would an uncompromising life look like for me?

What do I need to remove from my current life to make my life more authentic?

What is one bold action I can take right now that would allow me to express who I am more authentically in the world?

What is my true passion? What do I dream of?

AFFIRMATION:

I am devoted to the full expression of who I am. I defend and protect the story of my life. I know that when I am expressing myself, without hesitation or limitation, I AM the contribution that I am here to give the world. Being myself IS my Life Purpose and my direction flows from my authentic alignment.

EFT SETUP:

Even though I question whether I have something of value to add to the world, I now choose to courageously follow the whispers of my soul and live a life that is a powerful expression of the truth of who I am. I speak my truth. I value my contribution. I know I am precious, and I deeply and completely love and accept myself.

EARTH:

Gate 14: Creation

Ask yourself this week, "If I didn't need the money, what work would I be doing?" How is this work showing up in your life right now?

MAY 19, 2023
NEW MOON

 Taurus 28 degrees, 25 minutes

Gate 8: The Gate of Fulfillment

New moon energy invites us to explore how we can deepen our alignment with our intentions and asks us to focus on what we want to grow and expand on in our lives.

Before we take a look at this new moon, let's do a quick review of the lessons that the Moon has been giving us so far this year. From the beginning of the year, the Moon has been asking us to review how willing we are to be supported and collaborative. She's been inviting us to look at how much faith we have, how much are we willing to place our trust in the Universe and, because of that trust, how willing are we to be relentlessly authentic.

This new moon continues the theme by inviting us to dream of how our life would look if we were an uncompromisingly authentic expression of who we were born to be.

This new moon wants you to be relentlessly honest and pure in how you share your heart with the world. What do you want to grow and expand on in your life that would support you being completely aligned with your authentic self? What dreams have you been nurturing and maybe even hiding that are longing for you to birth into the world? What would your life look like if you were radically authentic? Now is the time to unleash your heart and show it to the world with courage and honesty.

CHALLENGE:

To learn to express yourself authentically. To wait for the right people to see the value of who you are, and to share yourself with them vulnerably with all your heart. To learn to trust that you are a unique expression of the Divine with a purpose and a path. To find that path and to walk it without self-judgment or holding back.

OPTIMAL EXPRESSION:

To push the edges and boundaries of authentic self-expression and to realize that you being the full expression of your authentic self IS your Life Purpose. To use your authentic expression to inspire others to fulfill themselves.

UNBALANCED EXPRESSION:

Feeling panicked and disconnected from your Life Purpose. Thinking that your Life Purpose is something you have to "do" versus someone you have to "be." To try to be someone you're not in an attempt to serve as a "role model."

CONTEMPLATIONS:

Do I feel safe being vulnerable? What experiences have caused me to feel unsafe expressing my true self? Can I rewrite those stories?

What would an uncompromising life look like for me?

What do I need to remove from my current life to make my life more authentic?

What is one bold action I can take right now that would allow me to express who I am more authentically in the world? What is my true passion? What do I dream of?

AFFIRMATION:

I am devoted to the full expression of who I am. I defend and protect the story of my life. I know that when I am expressing myself, without hesitation or limitation, I AM the contribution that I am here to give the world. Being myself IS my Life Purpose, and my direction flows from my authentic alignment.

MAY 21, 2023

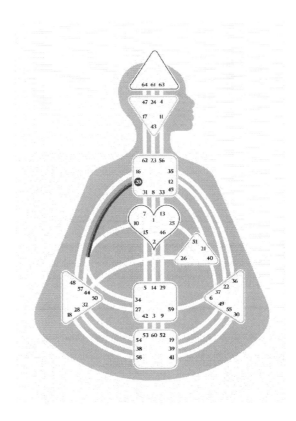

GATE 20: PATIENCE

CHALLENGE:

To be patient and control the ability to wait. To be prepared and watchful but resist the urge to act if the timing isn't right or if there are details that still need to be readied.

JOURNAL QUESTIONS:

How do I manage my need for action? Am I patient?

Do I trust in Divine Timing? Do I trust my intuition?

What needs to be healed, released, aligned, and brought to my awareness for me to trust Divine Timing?

What needs to be healed, released, aligned, and brought to my awareness for me to trust my intuition?

AFFIRMATION:

I am in the flow of perfect timing. I listen to my intuition. I prepare. I gather the experience, resources, and people I need that support my ideas and my principles. When I am ready I wait patiently, knowing that right timing is the key to transforming the world. My alignment with right timing increases my influence and my power.

EFT SETUP:

Even though it is scary to not *do* anything and wait, I now choose to trust the infinite abundance of the Universe, and I deeply and completely love and accept myself.

EARTH:

Gate 34: Power

How can you cultivate greater patience while you're waiting? What fears come up for you when you think of waiting? How can you learn to wait with patience and ease and see right timing as power?

MAY 27, 2023

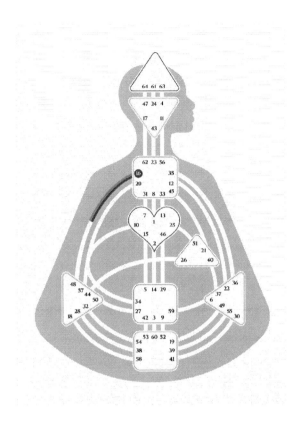

GATE 16: ZEST

CHALLENGE:

To learn to temper your enthusiasm by making sure you are prepared enough for whatever it is you are trying to do or create.

JOURNAL QUESTIONS:

Do I trust my gut?

Do I need to slow down and make sure I've done my homework before I take action?

Have I sidelined my enthusiasm because other people have told me that I cannot do what I dream of doing?

AFFIRMATION:

I am a faith-filled contagious force. I take guided actions and I trust my intuition and awareness to let me know when I am prepared and ready to leap into expanding my experience and genius. My enthusiasm inspires others to trust in themselves and to take their own giant leaps of growth.

EFT SETUP:

Even though I am afraid that I am not fulfilling my Life Purpose and am wasting my life, I now choose to relax and know that I am in the perfect place at the perfect time to fulfill my destiny, and I deeply and completely love and accept myself.

EARTH:

Gate 9: Convergence

This week explore your physical environment and ask yourself if there is something in your environment that is distracting you from your focus. What can you do to improve your environment? What can you do to increase your focus?

JUNE 2, 2023

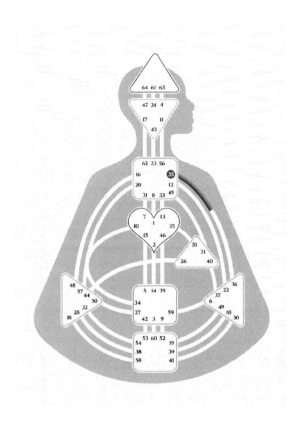

GATE 35: EXPERIENCE

CHALLENGE:

To not let experience lead to feeling jaded or bored. To have the courage to share what you know from your experience. To know which experiences are worth participating in. To let your natural ability to become accomplished at anything keep you from being enthusiastic about learning something new. To embrace that even though you know how to know, you don't know everything.

JOURNAL QUESTIONS:

Where am I finding passion in my life? Do I need to create or discover more passion in my life right now?

Do I share my knowledge and the stories of my experiences? Do I see the value of what I have to share?

What am I curious about? How can I expand on that curiosity?

AFFIRMATION:

I am an experienced, wise, and knowledgeable resource for others. My experiences in life have added to the rich tapestry that is the story of humanity. I share my stories with others because my experiences open doorways of possibility for others. My stories help others create miracles in their lives.

EFT SETUP:

Even though in the past I struggled to stay focused and move forward, I now trust myself to take the next steps on manifesting my dream. I am focused, clear, and moving forward, and I deeply and completely love and accept myself.

EARTH:

Gate 5: Consistency

Do something symbolic this week that represents order and establishing order in your life. Clean a closet, sort through your purse or wallet. A good week to take stock of your habits and explore what habits might need a little refreshing or tweaking.

JUNE 3, 2023
FULL MOON

 Sagittarius 13 degrees, 17 minutes

Gate 5: The Gate of Consistency

Full moon energy invites us to explore what we need to release and let go of in order to stay in alignment with our intentions.

There is a direct relationship between the story we tell about who we are and the habits and patterns we follow in order to continue to express your story into your world. If you're telling a story of limitation and lack, you probably have habits that reflect this story. If the story you're telling is one of expansion and possibility, you have probably cultivated habits that support your growth.

This full moon is shining a light on our personal narrative and the habits we've cultivated. Are you marrying the story you tell in your head about who you are and what you hope to create in your life with the actions and habits that support the manifestation of your story? What aspects of your story might be limiting what you're allowing yourself to create? What habits and patterns do you need to change to support the manifestation of your dreams? This full moon will help you align with habits that will help you fulfill the true story of Who You Are.

 CHALLENGE:

To learn to craft order, habits and rhythm that support alignment, connection and the flow of Life Force energy and the fulfillment of purpose. To succeed at staying in tune with consistent habits and alignment that support your growth and evolution no matter what is going on around you. Aligning with natural order and staying attuned to the unfolding of the flow of the natural world.

OPTIMAL EXPRESSION:

The ability to stay consistent with habits and choices that bring you closer to living true to who you are through alignment, and not overusing will power.

UNBALANCED EXPRESSION:

Life will seem like a constant struggle to stay connected and live habitually in a way that creates stability, sustainability, and a fulfilled expression.

CONTEMPLATIONS:

What do I need to do to create habits that fuel my energy and keep me vital and feeling connected to myself and Source?

What habits do I have that might not be serving my highest expression? How can I change those habits?

What kind of environment do I need to cultivate to support my rhythmic nature?

AFFIRMATION:

Consistency gives me power. When I am aligned with my own natural rhythm and the rhythm of life around me, I cultivate strength, connection with Source, and I am a beacon of stability and order. The order I hold is the touchstone, the returning point of Love, that is sustained through cycles of change. The rhythms I maintain set the standard for compassionate action in the world.

JUNE 8, 2023

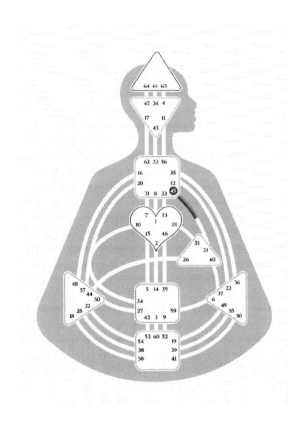

GATE 45: DISTRIBUTION

CHALLENGE:

To share and use your resources for the greater good of the whole. To learn to manage resources judiciously so that they benefit the greatest number of people. To teach as a pathway of sharing.

JOURNAL QUESTIONS:

Do I like to share? What do I have to give the world?

How do I own my right leadership? Am I comfortable as a leader?

Do I shrink from leadership? Do I overcompensate by pushing too hard with my leadership?

Do I trust that when the right people are ready, I will be pressed into action as a leader and a teacher?

What do I need to heal, release, align or bring to my awareness to trust my leadership energy more?

AFFIRMATION:

I am a teacher and a leader. I use my resources, my knowledge, and my experience to expand the resources, knowledge, and experiences of others. I use my blessings of abundance to increase the blessings of others. I know that I am a vehicle of wisdom and knowledge. I sense when it is right for me to share who I am and what I know with others.

EFT SETUP:

Even though I'm afraid to look at my finances, I now choose to take a real look at my financial numbers and know that awareness is the first step to increasing my financial status, and I deeply and completely love and accept myself.

EARTH:

Gate 26: Integrity

Where might you be experiencing a breach in your moral, identity, physical, resource or energetic integrity? What do you need to do to bring yourself back into integrity?

JUNE 14, 2023

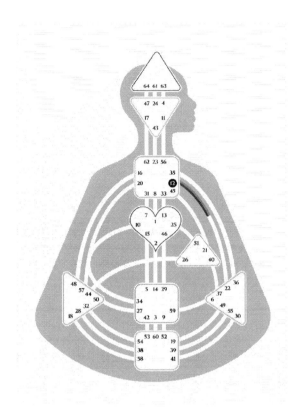

GATE 12: THE CHANNEL

CHALLENGE:

To honor the self enough to wait for the right time and mood to speak. To know that shyness is actually a signal that the timing is not right to share transformational insights and expressions. When the timing IS right, to have the courage to share what you feel and sense. To honor the fact that your voice and the words you offer are a direct connection to Source and you channel the potential for transformation. To own your creative power.

JOURNAL QUESTIONS:

How has shyness caused me to judge myself?

What do I need to do to cultivate a deeper connection with Source?

What do I need to do to connect more deeply with my creative power?

AFFIRMATION:

I am a creative being. My words, my self-expression, my creative offerings have the power to change the way people see and understand the world. I am a vessel of Divine Transformation and I serve Source through the words that I share. I wait for the right timing, and when I am aligned with timing and flow, my creativity creates beauty and grace in the world. I am a Divine Channel, and I trust that the words that I serve will open the Hearts of others.

EFT SETUP:

Even though I am afraid that I am failing my Life Purpose and mission, I now choose to know that I am in the right place fulfilling my right purpose. All I need to do is to follow my Strategy, be deliberate, follow my heart, and all will be exactly as it needs to be, and I deeply and completely love and accept myself.

EARTH:

Gate 11: The Conceptualist

Get a blank notebook and train yourself to get into the habit of writing down all of your ideas. Nurture these ideas. Dream about them. Fantasize about them and see what shows up in your life in response.

JUNE 17, 2023
NEW MOON

 Gemini 26 degrees, 42 minutes

Gate 12: The Gate of The Channel

New Moon energy invites us to explore how we can deepen our alignment with our intentions and asks us to focus on what we want to grow and expand on in our lives.

This new moon brings the sweet energy of inspiration. Be prepared this week for downloads, a multitude of new ideas and the emergence of new ways to implement these ideas. Be sure to carry around a notebook with you all week as you might need to capture these ideas.

Remember that not all ideas that come to you are yours to fulfill. Some of your new ideas are for you to share with others. Some are for you. Pay attention to the new ideas that stir your excitement and your passion. Your emotional response to these new ideas gives you clues as to which ideas are yours to nurture and manifest.

The next few months promise to bring innovation and the fulfillment of potential. Remember that gratitude is essential for growth. Before you leap into a new idea, remember to notice what is working in your life so that you can continue to expand upon your blessings.

 CHALLENGE:

To honor the self enough to wait for the right time and mood to speak. To know that shyness is actually a signal that the timing isn't right to share your transformational insights and expressions. When the timing IS right, to have the courage to share what you feel and sense. To honor the fact that your voice and the words you offer are a direct connection to Source and you channel the potential for transformation. To own your creative power.

OPTIMAL EXPRESSION:

To know that your voice is an expression of transformation and a vehicle for Divine Insight. The words you speak, the insights and creativity you share have the power to change others and the world. This energy is so powerful that people have to be ready to receive it. When you are able to articulate, it means timing is correct. If you struggle to find the words, have the courage to wait until it feels more aligned. A powerful ability to craft language and creative expressions that changes people's perceptions.

UNBALANCED EXPRESSION:

The struggle to try to speak ideas into form when it's not the right time. Letting hesitancy and caution paralyze you. Trying to force ideas and words.

CONTEMPLATIONS:

How has "shyness" caused me to judge myself?

What do I need to do to cultivate a deeper connection with Source?

What do I need to do to connect more deeply with my creative power?

AFFIRMATION:

I am a creative being. My words, my self-expression, my creative offerings have the power to change the way people see and understand the world. I am a vessel of Divine Transformation and I serve Source through the words that I share. I wait for the right timing and when I am aligned with timing and flow, my creativity creates beauty and grace in the world. I am a Divine Channel and I trust that the words I serve will open the Hearts of others.

JUNE 20, 2023

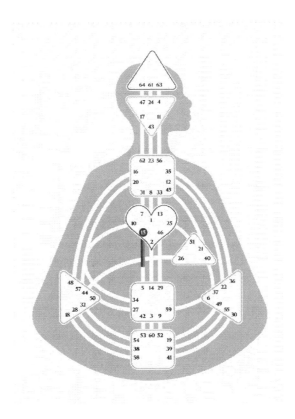

GATE 15: COMPASSION

CHALLENGE:

To learn to allow yourself to be in the flow of your own rhythm. To not beat yourself up because you don't have daily habits. To have the courage to do the right thing even if you are worried about not having enough. To share from the heart without giving up your heart, serving as a martyr.

JOURNAL QUESTIONS:

Do I trust my own rhythm?

Do I share from the heart?

Do I over-share

Does my sharing compromise my own heart?

Do I judge my own rhythm?

Can I find peace in aligning with my own rhythm?

What old patterns do I need to break?

AFFIRMATION:

Like the power of a hurricane to transform the shoreline, my unique rhythm brings change to the landscape of my life and the world around me. I embrace my own rhythm and acknowledge the power of my own heart. I share with ease, and I serve my own heart as the foundation of all I have to give the world.

EFT SETUP:

Even though I feel powerless to make a difference in the world, I now choose to follow my heart and my passion, knowing I am the greatest gift I can give the world. The more I show up as my true self, the more I empower others to do the same, and I deeply and completely love and accept myself.

EARTH:

Gate 10: Self-Love

This week focus on nurturing yourself. What can you do to express love and appreciation for yourself?

JUNE 26, 2023

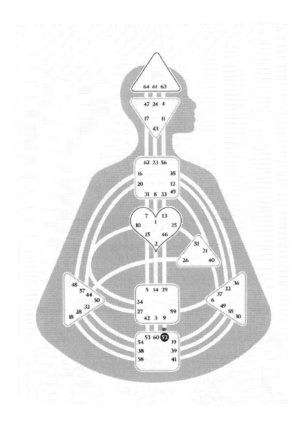

GATE 52: PERSPECTIVE

CHALLENGE:

To learn to stay focused even when you're overwhelmed by a bigger perspective. To see the big picture, to not let the massive nature of what you know confuse you and cause you to struggle with where to put your energy and attention.

JOURNAL QUESTIONS:

What do I do to maintain and sustain my focus?

Is there anything in my environment or my life that I need to move out of the way for me to deepen my focus?

How do I manage feeling overwhelmed?

What things am I avoiding because I feel overwhelmed by them?

What is one bold action I can take to begin clearing the path for action?

How does my feeling of being overwhelmed affect my self-worth?

How can I love myself more deeply despite feeling overwhelmed?

AFFIRMATION:

I am like the eagle soaring above the land. I see the entirety of what needs to happen to facilitate the evolution of the world. I use my perspective to see my unique and irreplaceable role in the Cosmic Plan. I see relationships and patterns that others do not always see. My perspective helps us build a peaceful world more effectively and in a consciously directed way.

EFT SETUP:

Even though it makes me nervous to stop *doing* and sit with the stillness, I now trust the process and know that my state of alignment and clarity with my intentions is the most powerful thing I can do to create effectively and powerfully in my life. I relax, I trust and let my abundance unfold, and I deeply and completely love and accept myself.

EARTH:

Gate 58: Joy

Do at least five things this week simply for the joy of it. Notice how joy feels and commit to cultivating more joy in your daily practice.

JULY 2, 2023

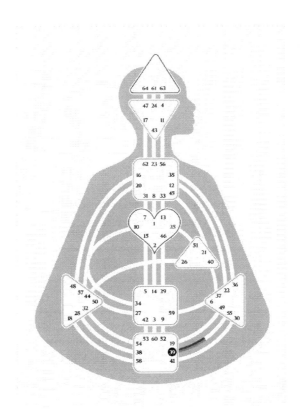

GATE 39: RECALIBRATION

CHALLENGE:

To challenge and tease out energies that are not in alignment with faith and abundance. To bring them to awareness and to use them as pushing off points to deepen faith and trust in Source.

JOURNAL QUESTIONS:

Do I trust Source?

What do I need to do to deepen my trust in Source?

Do I feel like I am enough?

Do I feel like I have enough?

Take stock of everything you have and everything you've been given. Do I have enough? Have I ever not been supported?

What do I have that I'm grateful for?

Have I abdicated my own power to create?

What needs to be healed, released, aligned, or brought to my awareness to reactivate my power to create my own abundance?

AFFIRMATION:

I am deeply calibrated with my faith. I trust that I am fully supported. I use experiences that create desire and want in me as opportunities to deepen the faith that I will receive and create all that I need to fulfill my mind, body, and spirit. I am in the perfect flow of abundance, and I am deeply aligned with Source.

EFT SETUP:

Even though I worry about money, having the right relationship, and creating abundance in every area of my life, I now trust Spirit and allow the abundant nature of the Universe to reveal itself to me. I stay open to the possibilities of miracles and trust that all I have to do is stay conscious of the abundance of Spirit unfolding within me, and I deeply and completely love and accept myself.

EARTH:

Gate 38: The Visionary

One of the biggest things that can shut you down and cause you to procrastinate is not having a big enough dream. If you were going to blow the edges and limitations off your dream, what would you create with your life? What is your really, *really* big dream? Spend some time imagining the fulfillment of your dream this week.

JULY 3, 2023
FULL MOON

♑ **Capricorn 11 degrees, 18 minutes**
Gate 38: The Gate of the Visionary

Full moon energy invites us to explore what we need to release and let go of to stay in alignment with our intentions.

This full moon is helping us explore our limitations and to let go of all those places where we've settled and down-sized our dream because it felt unattainable or too hard. We are being encouraged to recalibrate ourselves toward our big dreams and not settle for less than what we want because we believe it's not possible.

If you've been procrastinating and avoiding, or if you feel disconnected from the joy of creating, it might be that you've down-sized your dream to such a degree that it doesn't inspire or excite you anymore. Sometimes to unleash your energy and drive, you have to dream bigger, not smaller.

What needs to be healed, released, aligned, and brought to your awareness for you to re-imagine your dream so that it is big enough, unlimited enough and inspiring enough to drive you forward?

 CHALLENGE:

To experience challenge as a way of knowing what's worth fighting for. To turn the story of struggle into a discovery of meaning and to let the power of what you discover serve as a foundation for a strong vision of transformation that brings dreams into manifested form.

OPTIMAL EXPRESSION:

The ability to know what's worth committing to and fighting for. To use your experiences to craft a vision that anchors the possibility of something truly meaningful and worthy in the world. Serving the world as a visionary.

UNBALANCED EXPRESSION:

To struggle and fight for the sake of fighting. Engaging in meaningless fights. Aggression and struggle.

CONTEMPLATIONS:

Do I know what's worth committing to and fighting for in my life?

Do I have a dream that I am sharing with the world?

Do I know how to use my struggles and challenges as the catalyst for creating deeper meaning in the world? In my life?

AFFIRMATION:

My challenges, struggles and adventures have taught me about what is truly valuable in life. I use my understandings to hold a vision of what else is possible for the world. I am aligned with the values that reflect the preciousness of life and I sustain a vision for a world that is aligned with heart. My steadfast commitment to my vision inspires others to join me in creating a world of equitable, sustainable peace.

JULY 7, 2023

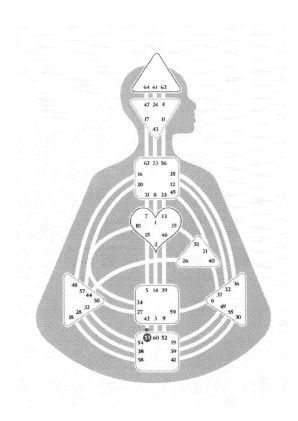

GATE 53: STARTING

CHALLENGE:

To respond in alignment with your energy blueprint to opportunities to get things started. To initiate the process of preparing or setting the stage for the manifestation of a dream before it becomes a reality. To learn to trust in the timing of the Universe and not take charge and try to implement your own ideas while working against Divine Timing. To not burn out trying to complete things. To find peace as a "starter," not a "finisher."

JOURNAL QUESTIONS:

How do I feel about myself when I have an idea and I can't get it initiated?

How do I feel when someone takes my initial idea and builds on it?

Do I value what I started?

What identities and attachments do I have to being the one who starts and finishes something?

Do I judge myself for not finishing something?

How can I be gentler with myself?

Do I trust Divine Timing?

How can I deepen my trust in right timing?

 ## AFFIRMATION:

I am a servant to Divine Inspiration. My thoughts, inspirations, and ideas set the stage for creative expansion and the potential for evolution. I act on the ideas that present themselves to me in an aligned way. I honor all other ideas, knowing that my gift is in the spark of energy that gets things rolling when the timing is right. While I wait for right timing, I guard my energy and charge my battery so that I am sustainable when the time is right for action.

 ## EFT SETUP:

Even though I am scared to believe that my big dreams could come true, I now choose to trust the infinite power of the Universe and know that I am never given a dream that can't be fulfilled, and I deeply and completely love and accept myself.

 ## EARTH:

Gate 54: Divine Inspiration

Is there anything you need to do or prepare to be ready for the next step in manifesting your dream or inspiration?

JULY 13, 2023

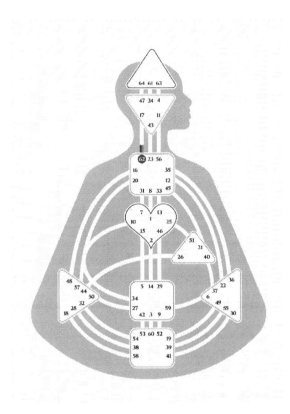

GATE 62: PREPARATION

CHALLENGE:

To trust that you will be prepared for the next step. To not let worry and over-preparation distract you from being present in the moment. To let the fear of not being ready keep you trapped.

JOURNAL QUESTIONS:

Do I worry? What do I do to manage my worry?

What can I do to trust that I know what I need to know?

What proof do I have that I am in the flow of preparation?

Is there anything in my life right now that I need to plan for?

Am I over-planning? Does my need for contingency plans keep me stuck?

AFFIRMATION:

I create the foundation for the practice of excellence by engineering the plan of action that creates growth. I am in the flow of my understanding, and I use my knowledge and experience to be prepared for the evolution of what is next. I am ready and I am prepared. I trust my own preparation and allow myself to be in the flow of what is next knowing that I will know what I need to know when I need to know it.

EFT SETUP:

Even though I feel pressure to do something, I now choose to relax and trust the power of my dreams to call the right circumstance to me, and I deeply and completely love and accept myself.

EARTH:

Gate 61: Wonder

This week, take some time to look up at the sky. Go somewhere where you can see the stars if possible and gaze at the face of the Cosmos with awe. Bring the feeling of awe into your everyday life.

JULY 17, 2023
NEW MOON

 Cancer 24 degrees, 55 minutes

Gate 62: The Gate of Preparation

New Moon energy invites us to explore how we can deepen our alignment with our intentions and asks us to focus on what we want to grow and expand on in our lives.

This new moon arrives with a "plan" in her hands. The darkness of this new moon invites us to draw inward and explore the next practical steps we need to take to be prepared for the fulfillment of our ideas. Take some time with this new moon and think about what actions you can take while you are incubating your big dream. What foundational actions can you do to prepare the way for the next right step in the fulfillment of your idea.

When you are prepared, you create room for yourself to receive more. When you allow yourself to receive more, you expand upon what you have. When you expand upon what you have, you have more to share.

 CHALLENGE:

To trust that you'll be prepared for the next step. To not let worry and over-preparation detract you from being present to the moment. To let the fear of not being ready keep you trapped.

OPTIMAL EXPRESSION:

The ability to be attuned to what is necessary to be prepared, and to trust that your alignment will inform you of everything that you need. Relaxing and knowing that you'll know what you need to know when you need to know it.

UNBALANCED EXPRESSION:

Fear and worry. Over-preparation. Allowing the plan to override the flow.

CONTEMPLATIONS:

Do I worry? What do I do to manage my worry?

What can I do to trust that I know what I need to know?

What proof do I have that I am in the flow of preparation?

Is there anything in my life right now that I need to plan for?

Am I over-planning?

Does my need for contingency plans keep me stuck?

AFFIRMATION:

I create the foundation for the practice of mastery by engineering the plan of action that creates growth. I am in the flow of my understanding, and I use my knowledge and experience to prepare for the evolution of what's next. I am ready and I am prepared. I trust my own preparation and allow myself to be in the flow of what's next, knowing that I'll know what I need to know when I need to know it.

JULY 19, 2023

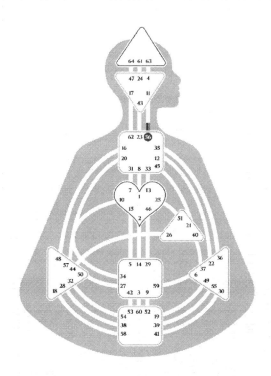

GATE 56: EXPANSION

CHALLENGE:

To learn to share stories and inspirations with the right people at the right time. To learn to tell stories of expansion and not depletion and contraction.

JOURNAL QUESTIONS:

What stories do I share repeatedly with others? Do they lift people up or cause them to contract?

What stories do I tell about myself and my voice? Do they cause me to expand or contract?

What am I here to inspire others to do or be?

AFFIRMATION:

I am a Divine Storyteller. The stories of possibility that I share have the power to inspire others to grow and expand. I use my words as a template for possibility and expansion for the world. I inspire the world with my words.

EFT SETUP:

Even though I'm afraid to share my ideas, I now choose to take leadership with my inspirations and share my precious ideas with others, and I deeply and completely love and accept myself.

EARTH:

Gate 60: Conservation

Gratitude is the gateway to transformation. This week take stock of everything in your life that IS good and that IS working. Make a daily list of the things you're grateful for.

JULY 25, 2023

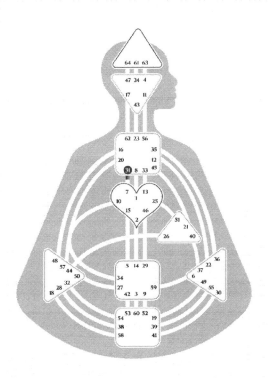

GATE 31: THE LEADER

CHALLENGE:

To learn to lead as a representative of the people you are leading. To cultivate a leadership agenda of service. To not let your fear of not being seen, heard, or accepted get in the way of healthy leadership. To learn to take your rightful place as a leader and not hide out.

JOURNAL QUESTIONS:

How do I feel about being a leader?

Am I comfortable leading?

Do I shrink from taking leadership?

What is my place of service? Who do I serve?

AFFIRMATION:

I am a natural born leader. I serve at my highest potential when I am empowering others by giving them a voice and then serving their needs. I use my power to lead people to a greater expansion of who they are and to support them in increasing their abundance, sustainability, and peace.

EFT SETUP:

Even though I'm afraid to be seen, I now choose to express myself and the magnificence that is me with gusto, courage, awareness of my own power and preciousness, and I deeply and completely love and accept myself.

EARTH:

Gate 41: Imagination

Your imagination is one of the most powerful creative tools you have access to. Spend time this week practicing using your imagination. What do you dream of? What other possibilities are there? Use your imagination to "see" other potential realities. You don't have to do what you imagine. Just use this power to stimulate creative emotional frequencies of energy.

JULY 31, 2023

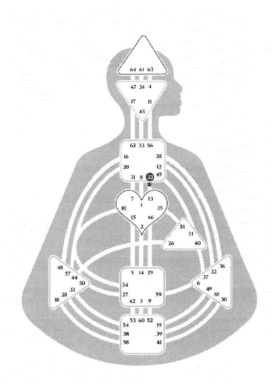

GATE 33: RETELLING

CHALLENGE:

To learn to share a personal narrative that reflects your true value and your worth. To share a personal narrative when it serves the intention to serve, improving the direction of others. To share history in an empowering way.

JOURNAL QUESTIONS:

What personal narratives am I telling that might be keeping me stuck, feeling like a victim, or feeling unlovable? How can I rewrite these stories?

What listening practices do I have? What can I do to listen better so that I can gauge when it is the right time to share in a powerful way?

AFFIRMATION:

I am a processor of stories. My gift is my ability to help others find the blessings, the love, and the power from stories of pain. I hold people's secrets and stories and transform them to share when the time is right. The stories I tell change the direction of people's lives. I use the power of stories to increase the power of heart in the world and to help build a world of Love.

EFT SETUP:

Even though the stories from my past have held me back, I now choose to rewrite the story of my life and tell it the way I choose; with forgiveness, embracing the gifts, and honoring my courage and strength in the story, and I deeply and completely love and accept myself.

EARTH:

Gate 19: Attunement

This week, spend some time alone in nature. Really feel how your energy feels in the restful embrace of the natural world. Practice "feeling" the energy of others and then contrasting it with your own energy so that you can better learn to distinguish your energy from the emotional energy around you.

AUGUST 1, 2023
FULL MOON

 **Aquarius 9 degrees, 15 minutes**
Gate 19: The Gate of Attunement

Full moon energy invites us to explore what we need to release and let go of in order to stay in alignment with our intentions.

This powerful full moon promises to be deeply emotional with a lot of potential for intensity and drama if we don't manage the energy effectively. The Moon is shining her light on our relationship agreements and invites us to explore whether our relationships are reflecting our value and values. If not, this is a powerful energy to help you rewrite and renegotiate your relationship contracts in a way that supports you and your partner in creating the intimacy and connection that you truly desire.

This full moon is asking us to explore our personal narrative and inviting us to rewrite any inner story we may be holding on to that is causing us to doubt our own lovability. What old wounds and experiences do you need to release or transmute in order to stay fully receptive to love and strongly proclaiming your value?

This energy is quite potent and, as I stated, potentially emotional. With this degree of emotional potential, be sure to take your time before you make any big decisions. At the same time, be sure you're not stalling and neglecting to have those difficult conversations that will ultimately help you create the love you deserve.

CHALLENGE:

To learn how to manage being a highly sensitive person and not let your sensitivity cause you to compromise what you want and who you are. To learn to keep your own resources in a sustainable state so that you have more to give. To not martyr yourself to the needs of others. To learn how to become emotionally intimate without being shut down or co-dependent.

OPTIMAL EXPRESSION:

The ability to sense the emotional needs of others and your community and know how to bring the emotional energy back into alignment with sufficiency and sustainability. The ability to be emotionally vulnerable and present, increasing Heart to Heart connections.

UNBALANCED EXPRESSION:

Being overly sensitive and shutting down or compromising your own needs and wants. Feeling disconnected from others as a way of coping with being overly sensitive. Being emotionally clingy or needy as a way of forcing your natural desire for intimacy.

CONTEMPLATIONS:

How do I manage my sensitivity?

What coping mechanism do I have to keep me emotionally connected in a healthy way?

Am I emotionally present in my relationships?

Do I need to become more attuned to my own emotional needs and ask for more of what I want and need?

What emotional patterns do I have that may be causing me to give up what I need and want to fulfill other people's emotional needs?

Am I able to be present to the emotional energy around me to help calibrate in a creative, intimate, and sustainable way?

AFFIRMATION:

I am deeply aware of the emotional needs and energy of others. My sensitivity and awareness give me insights that allow me to create intimacy and vulnerability in my relationships. I am aware and attuned to the emotional frequency around me and make adjustments to help support a high frequency of emotional alignment. I honor my own emotional needs as the foundation of what I share with others.

AUGUST 6, 2023

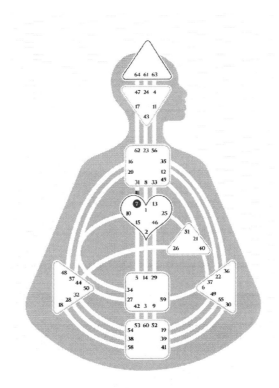

GATE 7: COLLABORATION

CHALLENGE:

To understand the need to be in front and allow yourself to serve through building teams, collaborating, and influencing the figurehead of leadership. To be at peace with serving the leader through support and collaboration. To recognize that the voice of the leader is only as strong and powerful as the support he or she receives.

JOURNAL QUESTIONS:

What are my gifts and strengths? How do I use those gifts to influence and lead others?

How do I feel about not being the figurehead of leadership?

What happens when I only support leadership? Do I still feel powerful and influential?

Make a list of the times when your influence has positively directed leadership.

AFFIRMATION:

I am an agent of peace who influences the direction and organization of leadership. I unify people around ideas. I influence with my wisdom, my knowledge, and my connections. I am a team builder, a collaborator, and I organize people in ways that empower them and support them in creating a collective direction rooted in compassion.

EFT SETUP:

Even though I feel confused and conflicted about what to do, I trust the Divine Flow and let the Universe show me the right thing to do at the right time, and I deeply and completely love, trust, and accept myself.

EARTH:

Gate 13: Narrative

Take some time this week to really listen to the story you're telling about who you are. Is it big enough? Are you taking control of your own story or are you allowing the past to define who you are? If you were going to rewrite your story, what would you say about yourself? How can you make your personal narrative truer to who you really are?

AUGUST 12, 2023

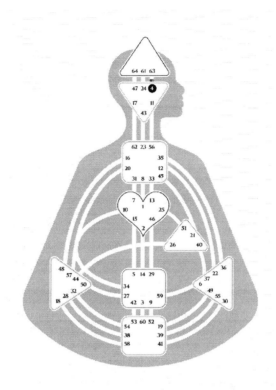

GATE 4: POSSIBILITY

CHALLENGE:

To learn to embrace ideas as possibilities, not answers, and to let the power of the possibility stimulate the imagination as a way of calibrating the emotions and the heart. This Gate teaches us the power of learning to wait to see which possibility actually manifests in the physical world, and to and to experiment with the options that come in response to those manifestations.

JOURNAL QUESTIONS:

What ideas do I have right now that need me to nurture and activate them?

What possibilities do these ideas stimulate right now? Take some time to write or visualize the possibilities.

Am I comfortable with waiting? What can I do to increase my patience and curiosity?

AFFIRMATION:

I am tuned into the Cosmic flow of possibility. I am inspired to explore new possibilities and potentials. I use the power of my thoughts to stretch the limits of what is known and engage my imagination to explore the potential of the unknown.

EFT SETUP:

Even though I don't know what to do, I allow my questions to seed the Universe, and I trust with great patience that the answers will be revealed to me, and I deeply and completely love and accept myself.

EARTH:

Gate 49: The Catalyst

Are you holding onto a situation for too long? Do you have a habit of quitting too soon? Is there a circumstance or condition in your life that you are allowing or running from because you fear the emotional energy associated with change? What needs to be healed or released?

AUGUST 16, 2023
NEW MOON

Leo 23 degrees, 16 minutes
Gate 4: The Gate of the Possibility

New Moon energy invites us to explore how we can deepen our alignment with our intentions and asks us to focus on what we want to grow and expand on in our lives.

If you've been grappling with trying to figure out a persistent question, be prepared to receive the answer this week. This new moon brings us the energy to create a revolution in our lives, to make big changes and to begin the process of implementing and exploring new possibilities.

Use this new moon to focus your energy on creating and calling in new opportunities and possibilities. This is not a time to figure out what's next, but to simply open your mind to new ideas and options. Use your imagination to explore new options with the awareness that the time you spend dreaming and contemplating is generating a critical mass of energy that will eventually manifest the answers you're seeking.

We are not in charge of time or timing, but we can influence it by giving energy to imagining new possibilities. The light of this new moon is helping you expand your creative options and encouraging you to allow your ideas to germinate in the matrix of your imagination.

CHALLENGE:

To learn to embrace ideas as possibilities, not answers, and to let the power of the possibility stimulate the imagination as a way of calibrating the emotions and the heart.

This Gate teaches us the power of learning to wait and see which possibility actually manifests in the physical world, and to and to experiment with the options that come in response to those manifestations.

This Gate also teaches us not to be doubtful if the idea isn't manifesting immediately or turn doubt inward if you can't figure out how to make this idea a reality.

 ## OPTIMAL EXPRESSION:

The ability to experience an idea as a possibility, to learn to use the idea as a "seed" for the imagination and to use the imagination to create an emotional response which then calibrates the Heart and attracts experiences and opportunities that match the possibility, into your life.

 ## UNBALANCED EXPRESSION:

Self-doubt and fear that you have an idea that you can't figure out. The pressure to try to share or implement the idea before it has had time to "seed" the manifestation. Acting too soon without waiting for the right timing.

 ## CONTEMPLATIONS:

What ideas do I have right now that need me to nurture and activate them?

What possibilities do these ideas stimulate right now? Take some time to write or visualize these possibilities.

Am I comfortable with waiting?

What can I do to increase my patience and curiosity?

 ## AFFIRMATION:

I am tuned into the Cosmic flow of possibility. I am inspired to explore new possibilities and potentials. I use the power of my thoughts to stretch the limits of what is known and engage my imagination to explore the potential of the unknown.

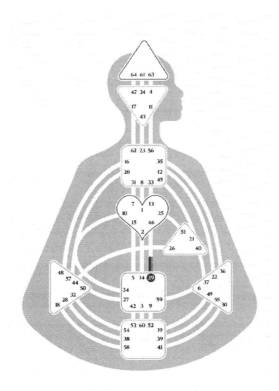

GATE 29: DEVOTION

CHALLENGE:

To discover what and who you need to devote yourself to. To sustain yourself so that you can sustain your devotion. To learn to say "no" to what you need to say no to, and "yes" to what you want to say yes to.

JOURNAL QUESTIONS:

What devotion do I have right now that drives me?

Is this a devotion that inspires me, or do I feel overly obligated to it?

Who would I be and what would I choose if I gave myself permission to say "no" more often?

What would I like to say no to that I am saying yes to right now?

What obligations do I need to take off my plate right now?

What would I like to devote myself to?

AFFIRMATION:

I have an extraordinary ability to devote myself to the manifestation of an idea. My commitment to my story and to the fulfillment of my intention changes the story of what is possible in my own life and for humanity. I choose my commitments with great care. I devote myself to what is vital for the evolution of the world, and I nurture myself first because my wellbeing is the foundation of what I create.

EFT SETUP:

Even though I am afraid to invest all my effort into my dream... what if it fails... what if I'm crazy... what if I just need to buckle down and be "normal"... I now choose to do it anyway, and I deeply and completely love and accept myself.

EARTH:

Gate 30: Passion

What do you need to do this week to sustain your vision or dream about what you are inspired to create in your life?

AUGUST 24, 2023

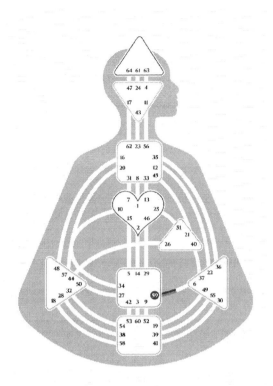

GATE 59: SUSTAINABILITY

CHALLENGE:

To learn to make abundant choices that sustain you, and at the same time, others. To collaborate and initiate others into sustainable relationships from a place of sufficiency. To learn to share what you have in a sustainable way.

JOURNAL QUESTIONS:

Do I trust in my own abundance?

How do I feel about sharing what I have with others?

Am I creating relationship and partnership agreements that honor my work?

Do I have relationships and agreements that are draining me? What needs to change?

How do I feel about being right?

Am I open to other ways of thinking or being?

Do I believe in creating agreements and aligning with people who have different values and perspectives?

AFFIRMATION:

The energy that I carry has the power to create sufficiency and sustainability for all. I craft valuable alliances and agreements that support me in expanding abundance for everyone. I hold to higher principles and values that are rooted in my trust in sufficiency and the all-providing Source. Through my work and alignments, my blessings serve to increase the blessings of myself and others.

EFT SETUP:

Even though I struggle to share my intentions, I now choose to boldly state them and wait for the pieces of my creation to magically fall into place, and I deeply and completely love and accept myself.

EARTH:

Gate 55: Faith

This week, deepen your experience of beauty. Surround yourself with beauty. Consciously bring beauty into your daily life and notice how abundantly beautiful life truly is.

AUGUST 29, 2023

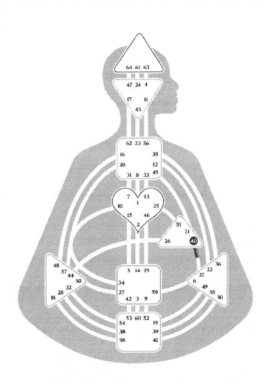

GATE 40: RESTORATION

CHALLENGE:

To learn to value yourself enough to retreat from community and the energy of those you love to restore, restock, and replenish your inner resources. To learn to interpret the signal of loneliness correctly. To take responsibility for your own care and resources and to not abdicate your own power to take care of yourself.

JOURNAL QUESTIONS:

What role does loneliness play in my life?

Has loneliness caused me to doubt my value?

What do I need to do to restore my energy?

Am I doing enough to take care of myself?

What agreements am I making in my relationships that might be causing me to compromise my value?

How can I rewrite these agreements?

Am I abdicating responsibility for my self-care?

Am I living a martyr model?

What needs to be healed, released, aligned, and brought to my awareness for me to take responsibility for cultivating my own sense of value and my self-worth?

AFFIRMATION:

I am a powerful resource for my community. The energy that I hold impacts others deeply and brings them to deeper states of alignment and sustainability. I take care of my body, mind, and soul because I know the more that I am and the more that I have, the more I can give to others. I take care of myself first because I know that good things flow from me. I am valuable and powerful, and I claim and defend the true story of Who I Truly Am.

EFT SETUP:

Even though it is hard to let go of the obligations of relationships, I now choose to release all relationships that are draining and unsupportive, and I deeply and completely love and accept myself.

EARTH:

Gate 37: Peace

When you feel that your outer world is chaotic and disrupted, how do you cultivate inner peace? Practice anchoring yourself in deep inner peace this week.

AUGUST 30, 2023
FULL MOON

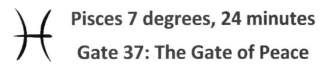 **Pisces 7 degrees, 24 minutes**
Gate 37: The Gate of Peace

Full moon energy invites us to explore what we need to release and let go of in order to stay in alignment with our intentions.

The Moon continues to bring us the theme of exploring our relationships and our relationship agreements. This full moon invites us to explore what bargains, deals and agreements we need to rewrite or renegotiate so that we can be at peace with ourselves and with each other.

This full moon wants you to release any resentments, attachment to broken agreements and to let go of any relationship dynamics that are not supporting you. You're also being invited to explore where things may be out of balance in your relationship, in particular resources and energetic investments.

It's also a good time to get really honest about asking for what you want and not projecting expectations and unspoken hopes. The key to making the most of this transit is to have clear, peaceful, and open conversations about what you want to co-create, and what agreements you need to make to get there together.

CHALLENGE:

To find inner peace as the true source to outer peace. To not let chaos and outer circumstances knock you off your center and disrupt your peace.

OPTIMAL EXPRESSION:

The ability to stay connected to sustainable peace and to respond to life by generating peace no matter what is happening in your external reality. Creating the emotional alignment necessary to make peaceful choices no matter what's going on in the outer world.

UNBALANCED EXPRESSION:

Desperately struggling to find peace outside of yourself. Trying to control the outer world to create inner peace.

CONTEMPLATIONS:

What habits, practices and routines do I have that cultivate my inner alignment with sustainable peace?

How do I cultivate inner peace when I feel that my outer world is chaotic and disrupted?

What do I need to do to cultivate a peaceful emotional frequency?

AFFIRMATION:

I am an agent of peace. My being aligned with peace creates an energy of contagious peace around me. I practice holding a peaceful frequency of energy and I respond to the world with an intention of creating sustainable peace.

SEPTEMBER 4, 2023

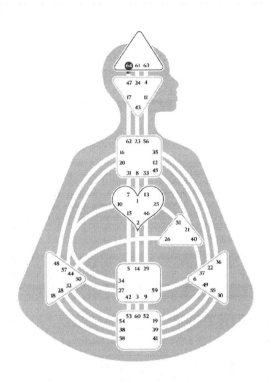

GATE 64: DIVINE TRANSFERENCE

 ### CHALLENGE:

To not let the power of your big ideas overwhelm you and shut down your dreaming and creating. To not get lost in the pressure of answering the "how?" question.

 ### JOURNAL QUESTIONS:

What do I do to take care of my big ideas?

How do I feel about having dreams but not always solutions?

How can I stop judging the gift of my dreams?

Do I trust that the "how" of my ideas will be revealed?

How can I deepen this trust?

AFFIRMATION:

I am a conduit for expansive thinking. My inspirations and ideas create the seeds of possibility in my mind and in the mind of others. I honor the dreams that pass through my mind and allow my big ideas to stimulate my imagination and the imagination of others. I trust the Universe to reveal the details of my dreams when the time is right. I use the power of my dreams to stimulate a world of possibility and expansion.

EFT SETUP:

Even though I don't know what is next, I wait and trust that the perfect right step will show up for me, and I deeply and completely love and accept myself.

Even though I feel overwhelmed with ideas, I trust the Universe to reveal the next step to me. I relax and wait, and I deeply and completely love and accept myself.

EARTH:

Gate 63: Curiosity

What needs to happen to release your attachment to being "right" and to allow yourself to dream of other possibilities? What if there's more than what you can see right now...?

SEPTEMBER 10, 2023

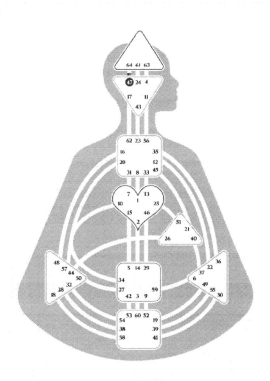

GATE 47: MINDSET

CHALLENGE:

To become skilled at a mindset of openness and possibility. To not let inspiration die because you don't know how to fulfill it.

JOURNAL QUESTIONS:

What thoughts do I have when I receive an idea or inspiration?

Am I hopeful or despairing?

How does it feel to let go of figuring out how I'm going to make my idea a reality?

What do I do to regulate my mindset?

What practices do I need to cultivate to increase the power of my thoughts?

AFFIRMATION:

My mindset is the source of my inspired actions and attitude. I know that when I receive an idea and inspiration it is my job to nurture the idea by using the power of my imagination to increase the potential and emotional frequency of the idea. I consistently keep my inner and outer environment aligned with the energy of possibility and potential. I know that it is my job to create by virtue of my alignment, and I relax knowing that it is the job of the Universe to fulfill my inspirations.

EFT SETUP:

Even though it is frustrating to not know how to make something happen, I now choose to wait for Divine Insight, and I trust that the right information will be revealed to me at the perfect time, and I deeply and completely love and accept myself.

EARTH:

Gate 22: Surrender

Where are you denying passion in your life? What is one thing you can do this week to reclaim your passion?

SEPTEMBER 14, 2023
NEW MOON

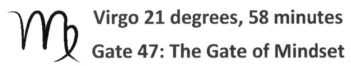 **Virgo 21 degrees, 58 minutes**

Gate 47: The Gate of Mindset

New Moon energy invites us to explore how we can deepen our alignment with our intentions and asks us to focus on what we want to grow and expand on in our lives.

The key to influencing what we create is learning how to regulate our mindset. We will create to the degree that we know how to relax, trust the process, and cultivate an attitude of faith and positive expectations while we wait.

The new moon invites us to explore and cultivate new habits, new ways of taking care of our mental health, while managing our attitude and expectations. It is easy, when we feel inspired by big ideas and dreams, to feel despair if we don't know how to make our dreams a reality.

The fulfillment of our dreams, including all the steps, synchronicity, and serendipity that need to transpire for us to continue constructing our dream, are not ours to figure out. If we force our mind to construct the "how" it limits the elegance and ease by which the Universe can make our dreams come true.

What new habits and patterns do you need to cultivate and commit to nurture and sustain a positive, open-minded, and faith-filled mindset?

CHALLENGE:

To master a mindset of openness and possibility. To not let inspiration die because you don't know how to fulfill it.

OPTIMAL EXPRESSION:

To engage in hopeful, inspired thoughts no matter what is going on around you. To use inspiration as a catalyst for calibrating emotional frequency and the Heart.

UNBALANCED EXPRESSION:

To quit or give up an inspiration because you can't figure out how to make it happen. To feel defeated and broken because you think you have ideas that you can't manifest.

CONTEMPLATIONS:

What thoughts do I have when I receive an idea or inspiration?

Am I hopeful or despairing?

How does it feel to let go of figuring out how I'm going to make my idea a reality?

What do I do to regulate my mindset?

What practices do I need to cultivate to increase the power of my thoughts?

AFFIRMATION:

My mindset is the source of my inspired actions and attitude. I know that when I receive an idea and inspiration, it is my job to nurture the idea by using the power of my imagination to increase the potential and emotional frequency of the idea. I consistently keep my inner and outer environment aligned with the energy of possibility and potential. I know that it is my job to create by virtue of my alignment and I relax knowing that it's the job of the Universe to fulfill my inspirations.

SEPTEMBER 16, 2023

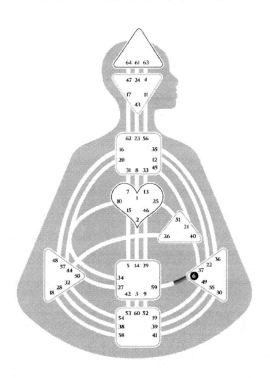

GATE 6: IMPACT

CHALLENGE:

To become proficient in using emotional energy and learn to trust that your impact is in service to the world. When you understand that your life is a vehicle for service and your energy is being used to influence and impact those around you, you assume greater obligation and responsibility to maintaining a high frequency of energy. The quality of the emotional energy you cultivate influences others to come together in an equitable, sustainable, and peaceful way. Learning to trust that your words and impact will have effect when the timing is correct and not overriding Divine Timing.

JOURNAL QUESTIONS:

What do I need to do to deepen my trust in Divine Timing?

What do I need to do to prepare myself to be seen and to have influence?

What do I need to do to sustain my emotional energy to align with peaceful and sustainable solutions?

How do I feel about lack? How do I feel about abundance? How can I create a greater degree of emotional abundance in my life and in my daily practice?

AFFIRMATION:

My emotional energy influences the world around me. I am rooted in the energy of equity, sustainability, and peace. When I am aligned with abundance, I am an energetic source of influence that facilitates elegant solutions to creating peace and well-being. I am deliberate and aligned with values that create peace in my life, in my community, and in the world.

EFT SETUP:

Even though I am ready to leap into action, I now choose to take a breath, wait out my emotions, and trust that the right timing will be revealed to me. I'm not missing out on anything. Divine Order is the rule of the day, and I deeply and completely love and accept myself.

EARTH:

Gate 36: Exploration

Go on a "miracle hunt" today. Make a list of all the unexpected synchronous and serendipitous events that have happened in your life. What has been the greatest miracle or unexpected event you've experienced in your life?

SEPTEMBER 21, 2023

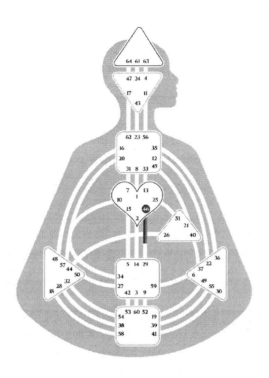

GATE 46: EMBODIMENT

CHALLENGE:

To learn to love your body. To learn to fully be in your body. To learn to love the sensual nature of your physical form and to move it with love and awareness.

JOURNAL QUESTIONS:

Do I love my body?

What can I do to deepen my love for my body?

What parts of my body do I love and appreciate?

Make a list of every part of my body that I love.

What do I need to do to amplify the Life Force I am experiencing in my body?

What kinds of devotion and commitment do I experience that help me harness greater amounts of Life Force in my body?

How can I deepen my commitment and devotion to my body?

 ## AFFIRMATION:

My body is the vehicle for my soul. My ability to fully express who I am (and my life and soul purpose) is deeply rooted in my body's ability to carry my soul. I love, nurture, and commit to my body. I appreciate all of its miraculous abilities and form. Every day I love my body more.

 ## EFT SETUP:

Even though it is hard for me to love my body, I now choose to embrace my amazing physical form and honor it for all the good it brings me, and I deeply and completely love and accept myself.

 ## EARTH:

Gate 25: Spirit

Do you have a regular practice that connects you to Source? How can you deepen this practice this week?

SEPTEMBER 27, 2023

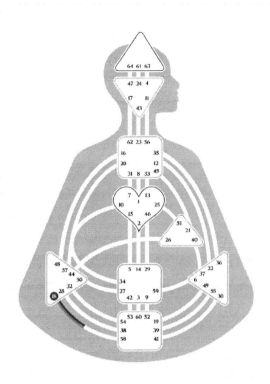

GATE 18: RE-ALIGNMENT

CHALLENGE:

To learn to wait for the right timing and the right circumstances to offer your intuitive insights into how to fix or correct a pattern. To wait for the right time and the right reason to share your critique. To understand that the purpose of re-alignment is to create more joy and not driven by a need to be right.

JOURNAL QUESTIONS:

What does joy mean to me? How do I serve it? How do I cultivate joy in my own life?

How does it feel to be right about something and keep it to myself?

Do I need to release any old stories about needing to be right?

Do I trust my own insights? Do I have the courage to share them when it is necessary?

AFFIRMATION:

I am a powerful force that re-aligns patterns. My insights and awareness give people the information they need to deepen their expertise and to experience greater joy. I serve joy and I align the patterns of the world and increase the world's potential for living in the flow of joy.

EFT SETUP:

Even though I feel criticized and judged, I now choose to hear the wisdom of the correction and release my personal attachment, and I deeply and completely love and accept myself.

EARTH:

Gate 17: Anticipation

What do you need to do to release any doubts and fears you may have about your own ability? What accomplishments do you have that you can celebrate and acknowledge?

SEPTEMBER 29, 2023
FULL MOON

♈ Aries 6 degrees, 00 minutes
Gate 17: The Gate of Anticipation

Full moon energy invites us to explore what we need to release and let go of in order to stay in alignment with our intentions.

This full moon is an invitation to remember the expansive power of your mind, and to create more by unleashing your imagination. You don't have to know exact details. Your thoughts are simply programming your mind to stay aware and curious about how to create what you want.

This full moon has the potential to be a little tricky. The high potential of this energy is the amplification of inspirations, thoughts, and ideas. The shadow of this energy is often expressed through opinion and seeing opinions as facts rather than potentials. Do your best during this energy to take everyone's opinions with a grain of salt and remember that perspectives are unlimited. Stay open-minded and know that the right next steps will reveal themselves to you when the timing is right.

What do you need to do to release your attachment to your ideas and to simply enjoy the experience of imagining all the potential options available to you?

 CHALLENGE:

To learn to share your thoughts about possibilities only when people ask for them. To not let doubt and suspicion keep you from seeing the potential of positive outcomes.

OPTIMAL EXPRESSION:

To use the power of your mind to explore potentials and possibilities that stretch our ideas about what else is possible in the human condition. To use your thoughts to inspire others to think bigger and bolder. To use your words to inspire and set the stage for creating energy that expands potential.

UNBALANCED EXPRESSION:

To share opinions that degrade options. To embrace opinions as truth and act on them. To create personal and collective narratives that are negative and filled with doubt.

CONTEMPLATIONS:

What do I need to do to manage my insights and ideas so that they increase the options and potential of others?

How do I feel about holding back from sharing my insights until the time is right?

What can I do to manage my need to share without waiting for right timing?

What routines and strategies do I need to cultivate to keep my perspectives expanding and possibility-oriented?

How can I improve my ability to manage doubt and fear?

AFFIRMATION:

I use the power of my mind to explore possibilities and potential. I know that my inspirations and insights create exploration and experimentation that can inspire the elegant solutions necessary to master the challenges facing humanity.

OCTOBER 3, 2023

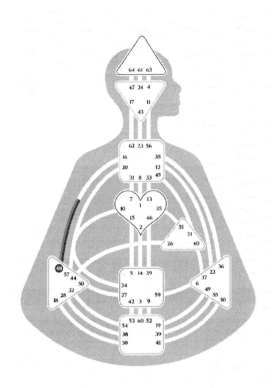

GATE 48: WISDOM

CHALLENGE:

To allow yourself to trust that you will know what you need to know when you need to know it. To not let the fear of not knowing stop you from creating. To *not* let not knowing hold you back.

JOURNAL QUESTIONS:

Do I trust my own knowing?

What needs to be healed, released, aligned, and brought to my awareness for me to deepen my self-trust?

What practice do I have that keeps me connected to the wisdom of Source?

How can I deepen my connection to Source?

AFFIRMATION:

I have a wealth of wisdom and knowledge. My studies and experiences have taught me everything I need to know. I push beyond the limits of my earthly knowledge and take great leaps of faith based on my deep connection to Source, knowing that I will always know what I need to know when I need to know it.

EFT SETUP:

Even though I am afraid I am not ready, I now choose to courageously dive in and just do it, and I deeply and completely love and accept myself.

EARTH:

Gate 21: Self-Regulation

How can you be more generous with yourself this week? How can you create an inner and outer environment that is more self-generous?

OCTOBER 9, 2023

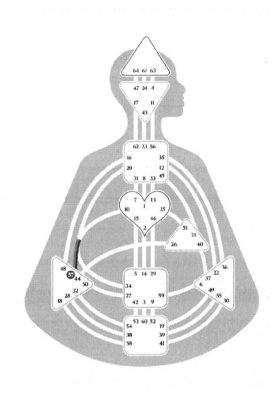

GATE 57: INSTINCT

CHALLENGE:

To learn to trust your own insights and gut. To learn to tell the difference between an instinctive response versus a fear of the future. To become skilled at connecting to your sense of right timing.

JOURNAL QUESTIONS:

Do I trust my intuition?

What does my intuition feel like to me?

Sometimes doing a retrospective analysis of your intuition and instinct makes it more clear how your intuitive signal works. What experiences in the past have I had where I knew what I should or should not do?

How have I experienced my intuition in the past?

When I think about moving forward in my life, do I feel afraid?

What am I afraid of? What can I do to mitigate the fear?

What impulses am I experiencing that are telling me to prepare for what is next in my life?

Am I acting on my impulses? Why or why not?

AFFIRMATION:

My Inner Wisdom is deeply connected to the pulse of Divine Timing. I listen to my Inner Wisdom and follow my instinct. I know when and how to prepare for the future. I take guided action and I trust myself and Source.

EFT SETUP:

Even though it is scary to trust my gut, I now choose to honor my awareness, quiet my mind, and go with what feels right, and I deeply and completely love and accept myself.

EARTH:

Gate 51: Initiation

What lessons have unexpected events brought into your life? Make note of how resilient you are.

OCTOBER 14, 2023

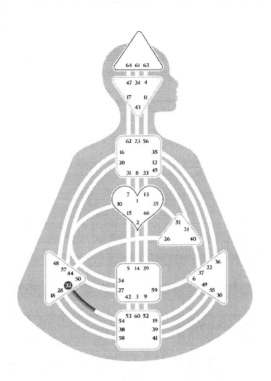

GATE 32: ENDURANCE

CHALLENGE:

To trust in Divine Timing. To prepare for the next step of manifestation and to align with the unfolding of the process. To be patient.

JOURNAL QUESTIONS:

What do I need to do to be prepared to manifest my vision?

What actionable steps need to be completed for me to be ready when the timing is right?

What do I need to do to cultivate patience?

Do I have a fear of failing that is causing me to avoid being prepared?

Am I over-doing and being overly prepared?

Am I pushing too hard?

What can I let go of?

AFFIRMATION:

I am a Divine translator for Divine Inspiration. I sense and know what needs to be prepared on the earthly plane to be ready for right timing. I am aligned with right timing, and I prepare and wait patiently knowing that when the time is right, I am ready to do the work to help transform pain into power.

EFT SETUP:

Even though I have worked hard to make my dreams come true and nothing has happened yet, I trust in Divine Timing and keep tending to my vision, and I deeply and completely love and accept myself.

EARTH:

Gate 42: Conclusion

To get the most of this week, explore what unfinished business you need to conclude. Are there things you need to say? Situations you need to end and be done with? Endings make room for new beginnings...

OCTOBER 14, 2023
NEW MOON/ANNULAR SOLAR ECLIPSE

 Libra 21 degrees, 07 minutes/ Libra 21 degrees, 10 minutes
Gate 32: The Gate of Endurance

New Moon energy invites us to explore how we can deepen our alignment with our intentions and asks us to focus on what we want to grow and expand on in our lives.

Eclipse energy amplifies the intensity of the new moon.

This is the last solar eclipse on the Taurus/Scorpio axis setting us up to do the work to begin the construction of the foundation of our dreams. The work and intentions we set into motion with this new moon promise to be fulfilled over the next three years.

This extra powerful new moon brings a conundrum of sorts. Be prepared for a certain quality of "push-me-pull-you" energy that might leave you feeling like you're all revved up with no place to go.

The energy of this new moon is activated when we trust in our future vision and connect with Divine Inspiration. The challenge is to divorce yourself from your expectations around time and timing.

This new moon encourages us to transcend our fear of failure and not let our fear of failure cause us to procrastinate doing the work we need to do to build the foundation for our dreams. We are being called to prepare the way for the manifestation of our future.

The Moon and the eclipse assure us that, if we create the energetic alignment and do the physical work necessary, we'll be ready to launch into massive expansion when the timing is right. Of course, the opposite is also true.

What work do you need to do to build the foundation for your dreams? Now is the time to commit to getting it done.

 ## CHALLENGE:

To trust in Divine Timing. To prepare for the next step of manifestation and to align with the unfolding of the process. To be patient.

 ## OPTIMAL EXPRESSION:

The awareness of what needs to be done to make a dream a manifested reality. Setting the stage, preparing, and being ready. The patience to trust that once the stage is set, the timing will unfold as needed to serve the highest good of all. To translate Divine Inspiration into readiness.

 ## UNBALANCED EXPRESSION:

Letting the fear of failure cause you to avoid preparing what you need to do. To not be ready when the timing is right. To push too hard, too fast, or too long against right timing.

 ## CONTEMPLATIONS:

What do I need to do to be prepared to manifest my vision? What actionable steps need to be completed for me to be ready when the timing is right?

What do I need to do to cultivate patience?

Do I have a fear of failing that is causing me to avoid being prepared?

Am I over-doing and being overly prepared? Am I pushing too hard? What can I let go of?

 ## AFFIRMATION:

I am a Divine translator for Divine Inspiration. I sense and know what needs to be prepared on the earthly plane in order to be ready for right timing. I am aligned with right timing, and I prepare and wait patiently, knowing that when the time is right, I will be ready to do the work to help transform pain into power.

OCTOBER 20, 2023

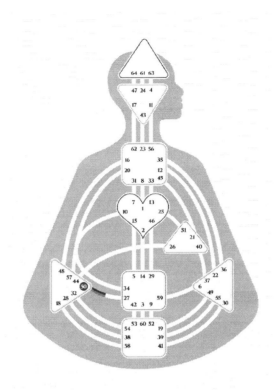

GATE 50: NURTURING

CHALLENGE:

To transcend guilt and unhealthy obligations and do what you need to do to take care of yourself in order to better serve others. To hold to rigid principles and judge others.

JOURNAL QUESTIONS:

How do I feel about taking care of myself first?

How do I sustain my nurturing energy?

What role does guilt play in driving and/or motivating me?

What would I choose if I could remove the guilt?

Do I have non-negotiable values? What are they?

How do I handle people who share different values from me?

AFFIRMATION:

My presence brings Love into the room. I nurture and love others. I take care of myself first to be better able to serve Love. I intuitively know what people need and I facilitate a state of self-love and self-empowerment by helping them align more deeply with the power of Love. I let go and I allow others to learn from what I model and teach. I am a deep well of love that sustains the planet.

EFT SETUP:

Even though it is hard for me to give and receive love, I now choose to be completely open to receiving and sharing deep and unconditional love, starting by deeply and completely loving and accepting myself first.

EARTH:

Gate 3: Innovation

What IS working in your life? Take some time to contemplate what aspects of your current reality you'd love to grow and expand upon.

OCTOBER 26, 2023

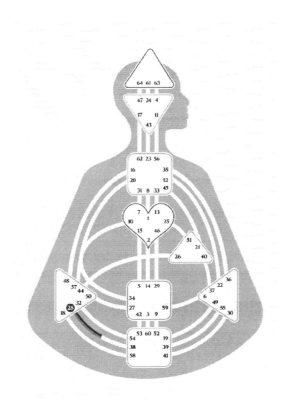

GATE 28: ADVENTURE/CHALLENGE

CHALLENGE:

To not let struggle and challenge leave you feeling defeated and desperate. To learn to face life as an adventure. To not let challenge and struggle cause you to feel as if you have failed.

JOURNAL QUESTIONS:

How can I turn my challenge into adventure?

Where do I need to cultivate a sense of adventure in my life?

What do I need to do to rewrite the story of my so-called failures?

What meanings, blessings, and lessons have I learned from my challenges?

What needs to be healed, released, aligned, and brought to my awareness for me to trust myself and my choices?

What do I need to do to forgive myself for my perceived past failures?

AFFIRMATION:

I am here to push the boundaries of life and what is possible. I thrive in situations that challenge me. I am an explorer on the leading edge of consciousness and my job is to test how far I can go. I embrace challenge. I am an adventurer. I share all that I have learned from my challenges with the world. My stories help give people greater meaning, teaching them what is truly worthy of creating, and inspire people to transform.

EFT SETUP:

Even though everything feels hard, I now trust that I am learning what is truly important in my life. I trust the lessons the Universe brings me, and I deeply and completely love and accept myself.

EARTH:

Gate 27: Accountability

Are you taking responsibility for things that aren't yours to be responsible for? Whose problem is it? Can you return the responsibility for the problem back to its rightful owner?

OCTOBER 28, 2023
FULL MOON/PARTIAL LUNAR ECLIPSE

 Taurus 5 degrees, 08 minutes/ Taurus 5 degrees, 03 minutes
Gate 27: The Gate of Accountability

Full moon energy invites us to explore what we need to release and let go of in order to stay in alignment with our intentions. Eclipse energy amplifies the intensity of the full moon.

This lunar eclipse is the last on the Taurus/Scorpio axis. This powerful eclipse axis, which began November 2021, has given us a deep exploration of our shadows and what needs to metaphorically die for us to be reborn and to gain momentum to move us forward into the future. We have been revising, restructuring, and exploring the depths of who we are, our purpose, and how to not limit ourselves in our creations in the world.

This final lunar eclipse on the Taurus/Scorpio axis highlights what we need to release to expand and evolve. If you've been doing your inner and outer work to build the foundation of your dreams, you are beautifully poised to do the work to make those dreams a reality.

This light of this fully moon/eclipse combination encourages us to let go of the things we cannot be responsible for, releasing any old obligations, responsibilities, and guilt that might be holding us back and exploring how we can build toward a dream that better embodies what we value and who we are. This is deep, powerful energy that penetrates the auras of others and invites us to work with each other in an equitable and sustainable way and get the work done.

We are exploring where we need to best take care of ourselves so that we can better take care of each other. We are looking at our goals and intentions with compassion and the ability to not only nurture ourselves but to use our own growth to better nurture and support those who are ready to grow.

We are setting the stage to create new infrastructures and systems that are rooted in compassion, high quality values, and the need to make sure that we take care of not only ourselves but each other.

 ## CHALLENGE:

To care without over-caring. To allow others to assume responsibility for their own challenges and choices. To learn to accept other people's values. To not let guilt cause you to compromise what is good and right for you.

 ## OPTIMAL EXPRESSION:

The ability to support, nurture, and lift others up. To sense and act on what is necessary to increase the wellbeing of others and the world. To feed people healthy food and healthy nourishment to ensure they thrive. To hold others accountable for their own self-love and self-empowerment.

 ## UNBALANCED EXPRESSION:

Co-dependency. Guilt. Over-caring. Martyrdom.

 ## CONTEMPLATIONS:

Am I taking responsibility for things that aren't mine to be responsible for?

Whose problem is it? Can I return the responsibility for the problem back to its rightful owner?

What role does guilt play in motivating me? Can I let go of the guilt?

What different choices might I make if I didn't feel guilty?

What obligations do I need to set down for me to take better care of myself?

Are there places where I need to soften my judgment of other people's values?

AFFIRMATION:

I have a nurturing and loving nature. It is my gift to love and care for others. I know that the greatest expression of my love is to treat others as capable and powerful. I support when necessary, and I let go with love so that my loved ones can discover their own strength and power.

OCTOBER 31, 2023

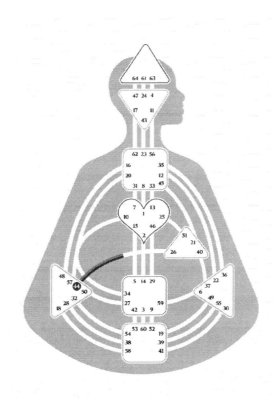

GATE 44: TRUTH

CHALLENGE:

To not get stuck in past patterns. To cultivate the courage to go forward without being stuck in the fear of the past. To learn how to transform pain into power and to have the courage to express your authentic self without compromising or settling.

JOURNAL QUESTIONS:

What patterns from the past are holding me back from moving forward with courage?

Do I see how my experiences from the past have helped me learn more about Who I Truly Am?

What have I learned about my value and my power?

What needs to be healed, released, aligned, and brought to my awareness for me to fully activate my power?

What needs to be healed, released, aligned, and brought to my awareness for me to step boldly onto my aligned and authentic path?

AFFIRMATION:

I am powerfully intuitive and can sense the patterns that keep others stuck in limiting beliefs and constricted action. Through my insights and awareness, I help others break free from past limiting patterns and learn to find the power in their pain and the blessings in their challenges and help them align more deeply with an authentic awareness of their True Value and Purpose.

EFT SETUP:

Even though it is hard for me to let go, I deeply and completely love and accept myself.

Even though I am afraid to repeat the past, I now move forward with confidence, trusting that I have learned what I needed to learn. I can create whatever future I desire, and I deeply and completely love and accept myself.

EARTH:

Gate 24: Blessings

Take some time to contemplate the hidden blessings in the painful events of the past. Can you find the bigger reason for why you've gone through what you've gone through?

NOVEMBER 6, 2023

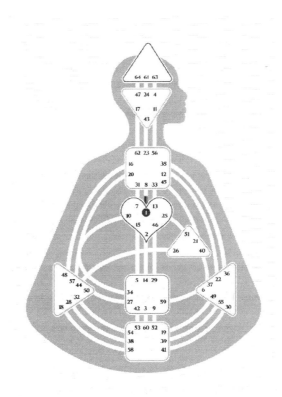

GATE 1: PURPOSE

CHALLENGE:

To discover a personal, meaningful, and world-changing narrative that aligns with a sense of purpose and mission: "I am…" To learn to love yourself enough to honor the idea that your life is the canvas, and you are the artist. What you create with your life IS the contribution you give to the world.

JOURNAL QUESTIONS:

Am I fully expressing my authentic self?

What needs to be healed, released, aligned, or brought to my awareness for me to deeply express myself authentically?

Where am I already expressing who I am?

Where have I settled or compromised? What needs to change?

Do I feel connected to my Life Purpose? What do I need to do to deepen that connection?

AFFIRMATION:

My life is an integral part of the cosmos and the Divine Plan. I honor my life and know that the full expression of who I am is the purpose of my life. The more I am who I am, the more I create a frequency of energy that supports others in doing the same. I commit to exploring all of who I am.

EFT SETUP:

Even though I am afraid that I am failing my life mission, I now choose to relax and allow my life to unfold before me with ease and grace. I trust that every step I take is perfectly aligned with my soul purpose, and I deeply and completely love and accept myself.

EARTH:

Gate 2: Allowing

How much good are you willing to allow into your life? Do you believe you can be fully supported?

NOVEMBER 12, 2023

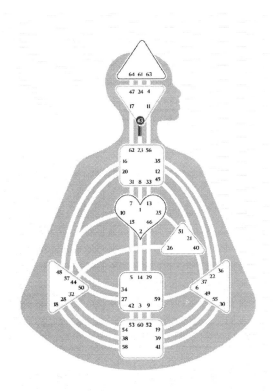

GATE 43: INSIGHT

CHALLENGE:

To be comfortable and to trust epiphanies and deep inner knowing without doubting what you know. To trust that when the timing is right you will know how to share what you know and serve your role as a transformative messenger who has insights that can change the way people think and what they know.

JOURNAL QUESTIONS:

Do I trust in Divine Timing?

Do I trust myself and my own Inner Knowing?

What can I do to deepen my connection with my Source of Knowing?

What needs to be healed, released, aligned, or brought to my awareness for me to trust my own Inner Knowing?

AFFIRMATION:

I am a vessel of knowledge and wisdom and have the ability to transform the way people think. I share my knowledge with others when they are ready and vibrationally aligned with what I have to share. When the time is right, I have the right words and insights to help others expand their thinking, recalibrate their mindset, and discover elegant solutions to the challenges facing humanity.

EFT SETUP:

Even though it is hard to wait for someone to ask me for my insights, I now choose to wait and know that my thoughts are valuable and precious. I only share them with people who value my insights, and I deeply and completely love and accept myself.

EARTH:

Gate 23: Transmission

Take stock of all the times you knew something even though you didn't know how you knew. Keep a running list of all your intuitive hits. Start affirming for yourself how reliable your knowingness is.

NOVEMBER 13, 2023
NEW MOON

♏ **Scorpio 20 degrees, 43 minutes**

Gate 43: The Gate of Insight

New Moon energy invites us to explore how we can deepen our alignment with our intentions and asks us to focus on what we want to grow and expand on in our lives.

This new moon pushes us into a cycle of transformation that starts with learning to trust our own insights and knowingness. Be prepared during this lunar cycle for deep insights and new knowledge to "drop in." The Moon promises to bring us new ways of seeing and knowing and invites us to trust our knowing, even if we don't know how we know what we know.

We are invited to give ourselves time to think and time to truly hear the inner whisperings of our wisdom and knowledge. The thoughts we have during this time might not be ready to be transmitted or shared. When the timing is right, others will know that we have the answers and insights they seek, and they will ask us for what we know. Until that time, we incubate our thoughts, feeling, sensing, and knowing.

There is great power in knowledge. The knowledge that we have that can transform the way people think and the perspectives they have is not necessarily knowledge gleaned from books or studies. This knowledge is given to us when we cultivate the internal and external environment necessary to receive and trust ourselves.

What do you need to do to ensure that you are cultivating an internal and external environment that supports you in being tuned into your own Inner Wisdom and Knowing?

CHALLENGE:

To be comfortable and to trust epiphanies and deep inner knowing without doubting what you know. To trust that when the timing is right, you will know how to share what you know and serve your role as a transformative messenger who has insights that can change the way people think and what they know.

OPTIMAL EXPRESSION:

The ability to tap into new knowledge, understanding, and insights that expand people's understanding of the world. To align with the right timing and trust that you'll know how to share what you know when you need to share it.

UNBALANCED EXPRESSION:

Feeling despair or frustration related to having knowledge but struggling to share what you know. Experiencing lightning bolts of knowingness and clarity but feeling overwhelmed by your inability to articulate what you understand. Not waiting for the right time to share what you know and feeling alone with your wisdom.

CONTEMPLATIONS:

Do I trust in Divine Timing? Do I trust myself and my own Inner Knowing? What can I do to deepen my connection with my Source of Knowing?

What needs to be healed, released, aligned, or brought to my awareness for me to trust my own Inner Knowing?

AFFIRMATION:

I am a vessel of knowledge and wisdom and have the ability to transform the way people think. I share my knowledge with others when they are ready and vibrationally aligned with what I have to share. When the time is right, I have the right words and the right insights to help others expand their thinking, recalibrate their mindset, and discover elegant solutions to the challenges facing humanity.

NOVEMBER 17, 2023

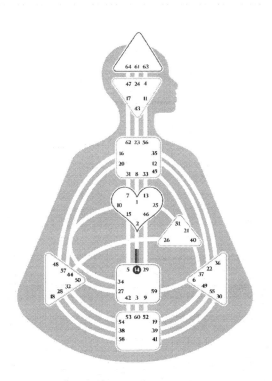

GATE 14: CREATION

CHALLENGE:

To learn to trust to respond to opportunities that bring resources instead of forcing them or overworking. To learn to value resources and appreciate how easily they can be created when you are aligned. To be gracious and grateful and not take the resources you have for granted.

JOURNAL QUESTIONS:

Do I trust that I am supported?

Am I doing my right work?

What is the work that feels aligned with my purpose?

How is that work showing up in my life right now?

What resources do I have right now that I need to be grateful for?

If I didn't need the money, what work would I be doing?

 ## AFFIRMATION:

I am in the flow of Divine Support. When I trust the generous nature of the Divine and I cultivate a state of faith, I receive all the opportunities and support that I need, to evolve my life and transform the world. I know that the right work shows up for me, and I am fulfilled in the expression of my Life Force energy.

 ## EFT SETUP:

Even though I am afraid I cannot do what I love and make money, I deeply and completely love and accept myself.

 ## EARTH:

Gate 8: Fulfillment

What would your life be like if you felt relentlessly authentic? Do one thing this week that is an authentic expression of who you are, without apology. Be bold.

NOVEMBER 23, 2023

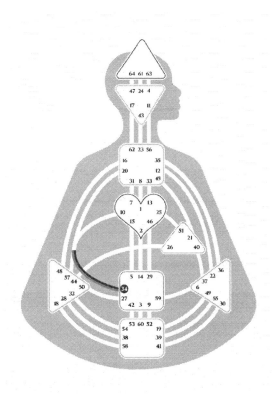

GATE 34: POWER

CHALLENGE:

To learn to measure out energy in order to stay occupied and busy but not burn yourself out trying to force the timing or the "rightness" of a project. To wait to know which project or creation to implement based on when you get something to respond to.

JOURNAL QUESTIONS:

Do I trust in Divine Timing?

What do I need to do to deepen my trust?

How do I cultivate greater patience in my life?

What fears come up for me when I think of waiting?

How can I learn to wait with greater faith and ease?

What do I do to occupy myself while I'm waiting?

AFFIRMATION:

I am a powerful servant of Divine Timing. When the timing is right, I unify the right people around the right idea and create transformation on the planet. My power is more active when I allow the Universe to set the timing. I wait. I am patient. I trust.

EFT SETUP:

Even though I am afraid to be powerful, I now choose to fully step into my power and allow the Universe to serve me while I serve it, and I deeply and completely love and accept myself.

EARTH:

Gate 20: Patience

How do you manage the pressure you feel around the need for action? What are constructive ways that you can bring yourself into harmony with right timing? What do you do while you're waiting for the timing to align?

NOVEMBER 27, 2023
FULL MOON

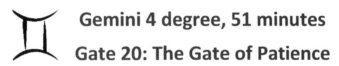 **Gemini 4 degree, 51 minutes**

Gate 20: The Gate of Patience

Full moon energy invites us to explore what we need to release and let go of in order to stay in alignment with our intentions.

This full moon gives us some powerful things to contemplate and release. The Moon has been giving us lessons about time and timing since October 14. We are not in charge of time but to influence time and be in alignment with right timing, we have to learn to honor the importance of it.

We are powerful when we are in alignment with the right time. If we are impatient, jump the gun, and move too fast out of a sense of urgency that is rooted in our own fear of not being or having enough, then we hemorrhage resources and fail to activate the full potential of our power.

The light of this full moon invites you to explore what you need to release in order to bring yourself into harmony with time and timing. How can you cultivate greater patience and trust? What do you need to heal, release, align, or bring to your awareness so that you trust and surrender to right timing?

 CHALLENGE:

To be patient and master the ability to wait. To be prepared and watchful but resist the urge to act if the timing isn't right, or if there are details that still need to be readied.

OPTIMAL EXPRESSION:

The ability to trust your intuition, to know what needs to be set in place, what people need to be gathered, what skills need to be mastered, and to be ready when the time is right. To trust in the right timing and to heed the intuition to get ready.

 ## UNBALANCED EXPRESSION:

To act before the time is right. To fail to listen to your inner guidance and prepare. To feel pressure to take action before the time is right, to feel frustrated, or to quit.

 ## CONTEMPLATIONS:

How do I manage my need for action? Am I patient? Do I trust in Divine Timing?

Do I trust my intuition?

What needs to be healed, released, aligned, and brought to my awareness for me to trust my intuition?

 ## AFFIRMATION:

I am in the flow of perfect timing. I listen to my intuition. I prepare. I gather the experience, resources, and people I need, to support my ideas and my principles. When I am ready, I wait patiently, knowing that right timing is the key to transforming the world. My alignment with right timing increases my influence and my power.

NOVEMBER 28, 2023

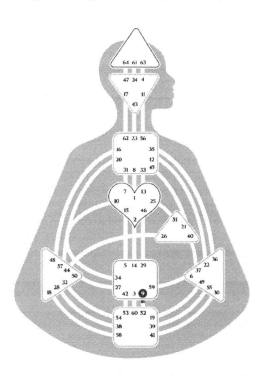

GATE 9: CONVERGENCE

CHALLENGE:

The energy is about learning where to place your focus. When we work with the energy of this Gate, we have to learn to see the trees AND the forest. This Gate can make us seem blind to the big picture and we can lose our focus by getting stuck going down a rabbit hole.

JOURNAL QUESTIONS:

Where am I putting my energy and attention? Is it creating the growth that I am seeking?

What do I need to focus on?

Is my physical environment supporting me in staying focused?

Do I have a practice that supports me sustaining my focus? What can I do to increase my focus?

AFFIRMATION:

I place my focus and attention on the details that support my creative manifestation. I am clear. I easily see the parts of the whole, and I know exactly what to focus on to support my evolution and the evolution of the world.

EFT SETUP:

Even though I have been frustrated with my lack of focus, I now choose to be clear, stay focused, and take the actions necessary to create my intentions.

EARTH:

Gate 16: Zest

Where have you sidelined your enthusiasm because others have told you that you can't do what you dream of doing?

DECEMBER 4, 2023

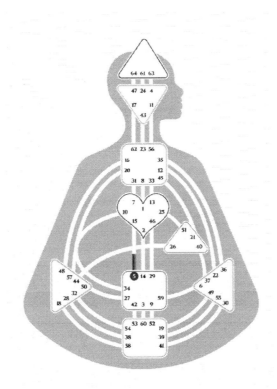

GATE 5: CONSISTENCY

CHALLENGE:

To learn to craft order, habits, and rhythm that support alignment, connection, and the flow of Life Force energy and the fulfillment of purpose. To become skilled at staying in tune with consistent habits and alignment that support your growth and evolution no matter what is going on around you. Aligning with natural order and staying attuned to the unfolding of the flow of the natural world.

JOURNAL QUESTIONS:

What do I need to do to create habits that fuel my energy and keep me feeling vital and connected to myself and Source?

What habits do I have that might not be serving my highest expression? How can I change those habits?

What kind of environment do I need to cultivate to support my rhythmic nature?

AFFIRMATION:

Consistency gives me power. When I am aligned with my own natural rhythm and the rhythm of life around me, I cultivate strength and connection with Source, and I am a beacon of stability and order. The order I hold is the touchstone, the returning point of love, that is sustained through cycles of change. The rhythms I maintain set the standard for compassionate action in the world.

EFT SETUP:

Even though I feel nervous/scared/worried about waiting for Divine Timing, I now choose to create habits that support my connection with Source while I wait, and I deeply and completely love and accept myself.

EARTH:

Gate 35: Experience

What experiences and stories from your own life do you have to share with others? Write a story about one of your favorite adventures you've experienced in your life. What did you learn? How has that shaped who you are?

DECEMBER 9, 2023

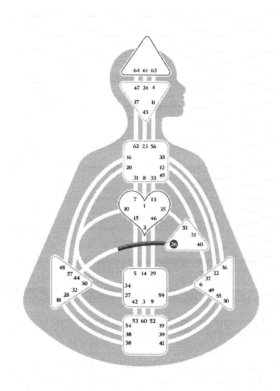

GATE 26: INTEGRITY

CHALLENGE:

To learn to value your right place and your value enough to act as if you are precious. To heal past traumas and elevate your self-worth. To trust in support enough to do the right thing and to nurture yourself so that you have more to give.

JOURNAL QUESTIONS:

Where might I be experiencing a breach in my moral, identity, physical, resource, or energy integrity?

What do I need to do to bring myself back into integrity?

Do I experience trauma when I act without integrity?

What trauma do I have that I need to heal?

How can I rewrite that story of my trauma as an initiation back into my true value?

What do I need to do right now to nurture myself and replenish myself to increase my sense of value?

AFFIRMATION:

I am a unique, valuable, and irreplaceable part of the Cosmic Plan. I am always supported in fulfilling my right place. I take care of my body, my energy, my values, and my resources so that I have more to share with the world. I claim and defend my value and fully live in the story of who I am with courage.

EFT SETUP:

Even though I am afraid to share my Truth, I now choose to speak my truth clearly and confidently, and I deeply and completely love and accept myself.

EARTH:

Gate 45: Distribution

This is a vital week to focus on what gifts you have to share with the world. How can you learn to give more without burning yourself out or martyring yourself? What do you need to do to increase your capacity to give and share?

DECEMBER 12, 2023
NEW MOON

 Sagittarius 20 degrees, 39 minutes

Gate 26: The Gate of Integrity

New Moon energy invites us to explore how we can deepen our alignment with our intentions and asks us to focus on what we want to grow and expand on in our lives.

This new moon brings us vital energy to prepare us for the new year! As we move closer to recalibrating for another journey around the Sun, we are doing the "homework" that sets the stage next year for us to put pedal to the metal and create what we truly want with the help of Saturn's guidance and support.

2024 continues to highlight the theme of faith. Faith, without a healthy sense of self-worth and a deep connection to your purpose, is hard to harness as a creative energy. When you don't value yourself and try to create without integrity for your authentic identity and your purpose, what you try to create can be twinged with desperation. When we don't believe that we are enough, we tend to create from an energy of not-enoughness and the essence of this internal sense of lack causes us to compromise our integrity.

This breach in integrity can impact the choices we make to sustain our physical health and wellness. We may hoard or overspend our money, compromise our authentic identity, act immorally or misuse our own energy. The result of being out of integrity with ourselves is depletion and burnout.

This new moon invites you to make a new commitment to your integrity. What daily actions, practices and habits do you need to take in order to heal your sense of value and to get yourself more aligned with your right place and purpose in the world?

CHALLENGE:

To learn to value your right place and your value enough to act as if you are precious. To heal past traumas and elevate your self-worth. To trust in Divine Support enough to do the right thing, and to nurture yourself so that you have more to give.

OPTIMAL EXPRESSION:

To live in moral, energetic, identity, physical and resource integrity with courage and trust. To set clear boundaries and take the actions necessary to preserve the integrity of your right place.

UNBALANCED EXPRESSION:

To compromise your integrity because you are afraid that you can't afford to fulfill your right place.

CONTEMPLATIONS:

Where might I be experiencing a breach in my moral, identity, physical, resource or energy integrity? What do I need to do to bring myself back into integrity?

When I am out of integrity, it can be traumatic. What trauma do I have that I need to heal?

How can I rewrite the story of my trauma as an initiation back into my true value?

What do I need to do right now to nurture myself and to replenish my value?

AFFIRMATION:

I am a unique, valuable, and irreplaceable part of the Cosmic Plan. I am always supported in fulfilling my right place. I take care of my body, my energy, my values, and my resources so that I have more to share with the world. I claim and defend my value and fully live the story of who I am with courage.

DECEMBER 15, 2023

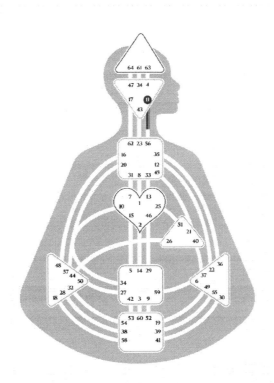

GATE 11: THE CONCEPTUALIST

CHALLENGE:

To sort through and manage all the ideas and inspiration you hold. To trust that the ideas that are yours will show up for you in an actionable way. To value yourself enough to value the ideas you have and to wait for the right people to share those ideas with.

JOURNAL QUESTIONS:

What do I do with inspiration when I receive it?

Do I know how to serve as a steward for my ideas or do I feel pressure to try to force them into form?

How much do I value myself? Do I value my ideas?

Do I trust the Universe? Do I trust that the ideas that are mine to take action on will manifest in my life according to my Human Design Type and Strategy?

What can I do to manage the pressure I feel to manifest my ideas?

Am I trying to prove my value with my ideas?

AFFIRMATION:

I am a Divine Vessel of inspiration. Ideas flow to me constantly. I protect and nurture these ideas knowing that my purpose in life is to share ideas and inspiration with others. I use the power of these ideas to stimulate my imagination and the imagination of others. I trust the infinite abundance and alignment of the Universe and I wait for signs to know which ideas are mine to manifest.

EFT SETUP:

Even though I have so many ideas, I now trust that I will know exactly what action to take and when to take it, and I deeply and completely love and accept myself.

EARTH:

Gate 12: The Channel

Spend some time this week contemplating what you need to do to deepen your connection with Source. Add some kind of creativity to your play and rest this week.

DECEMBER 20, 2023

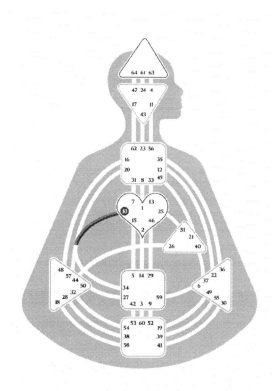

GATE 10: SELF-LOVE

CHALLENGE:

To learn to love yourself. To learn to take responsibility for your own creations.

JOURNAL QUESTIONS:

Do I love myself?

What can I do to deepen my self-love?

Where can I find evidence of my lovability in my life right now?

What do I need to do to take responsibility for situations I strongly dislike in my life right now? What needs to change?

Where am I holding blame or victimhood in my life? How could I turn that energy around?

AFFIRMATION:

I am an individuated aspect of the Divine. I am born of Love. My nature is to Love and be Loved. I am in the full flow of giving and receiving Love. I know that the quality of Love that I have for myself, sets the direction for what I attract into my life. I am constantly increasing the quality of love I experience and share with the world.

EFT SETUP:

Even though I struggle with loving myself, I now choose to be open to discovering how to love myself anyway, and I deeply and completely love and accept myself.

EARTH:

Gate 15: Compassion

Contemplate what old patterns in your life right now need to be healed and released. Take at least one grounded or symbolic way to commit to shifting and changing these patterns.

DECEMBER 26, 2023

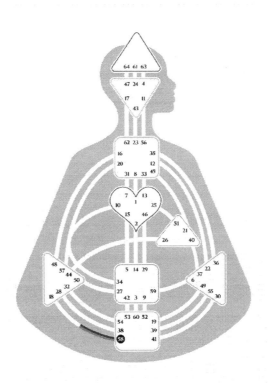

GATE 58: THE GATE OF JOY

CHALLENGE:

To follow the drive to create the fulfillment of your potential. To learn to craft a talent and make it consummate through joyful learning and repetition. To learn to embrace joy as a vital force of creative power without guilt or denial.

JOURNAL QUESTIONS:

What brings me the greatest joy?

How can I deepen my practice of joy?

How can I create more joy in my life?

What keeps me from fulfilling my potential and my talent?

What am I afraid of?

AFFIRMATION:

I am a consummate curator of my own talent. I use my joy to drive me to embody the fun expression of all that I am. I use practice as my path to excellency. I know that repetition and consistency create a more skillful expression of my talent. I embrace learning and growing, and I commit to the full expression of my joy.

EFT SETUP:

Even though it is hard to let go of the past, I now choose to release it and embrace all the joy that is available to me right now, and I deeply and completely love and accept myself.

EARTH:

Gate 52: Perspective

Is there anything in your environment or your life that you need to move out of the way for you to deepen your focus?

DECEMBER 26, 2023
FULL MOON

 Cancer 4 degree, 57 minutes

Gate 52: The Gate of Perspective

Full moon energy invites us to explore what we need to release and let go of in order to stay in alignment with our intentions.

Before an eagle can dive and catch their prey, they must first get a good view of the landscape below. This broad perspective helps them ensure that their actions are laser-focused and precise, using their energy effectively and with the intended results.

Focus and perspective are essential to influencing time and timing and also help us stay energized and aligned with our creative process. One of the ways that we can influence time and the quality of our efforts is to ensure that we are focused and that we don't get lost down rabbit holes that don't actually produce the results we're hoping for.

This full moon invites you to take stock of your environment and make sure you are creating an inner and outer environment that supports your focus and perspective. Are there things happening in your life that are distracting you from building what you truly want? How can you arrange your life, time, and energy so that you are more focused and precise with your efforts? What end results are you aiming for? How can you better simplify, delegate, or automate things in your life to create more room for focused action and calibration?

CHALLENGE:

To learn to stay focused even when you're overwhelmed by a bigger perspective. To see the big picture and to not let the massive nature of what you know confuse you and cause you to struggle with where to put your energy and attention.

OPTIMAL EXPRESSION:

The ability to see the bigger perspective and purpose of what is going on around you and to know exactly where to focus your energy and attention to facilitate the unfolding of what's next.

UNBALANCED EXPRESSION:

Attention deficit. To let overwhelm paralyze you and cause you to fail to act. To put your energy and attention in the wrong place and to spend your energy focused on something that bears no fruit.

CONTEMPLATIONS:

What do I do to maintain and sustain my focus?

Is there anything in my environment or my life that I need to move out of the way for me to deepen my focus?

How do I manage feelings of overwhelm? What things am I avoiding because I feel overwhelmed by them?

What is one bold action I can take to begin clearing the path for action?

How do my feelings of overwhelm affect my self-worth? How can I love myself more deeply, despite feeling overwhelmed?

AFFIRMATION:

I am like the eagle soaring above the land. I see the entirety of what needs to happen to facilitate the evolution of the world. I use my perspective to see my unique and irreplaceable role in the Cosmic Plan. I see relationships and patterns that others don't always see. My perspective helps us all to build a peaceful world more effectively and in a consciously directed way.

DECEMBER 31, 2023

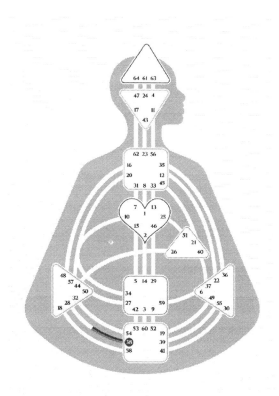

GATE 38: THE VISIONARY

CHALLENGE:

To experience challenge as a way of knowing what is worth fighting for. To turn the story of struggle into a discovery of meaning and to let the power of what you discover serve as a foundation for a strong vision of transformation that brings dreams into manifested form.

JOURNAL QUESTIONS:

Do I know what is worth committing to and fighting for in my life?

Do I have a dream that I am sharing with the world?

Do I know how to use my struggles and challenges as the catalyst for creating deeper meaning in the world and in my life?

AFFIRMATION:

My challenges, struggles, and adventures have taught me about what is truly valuable in life. I use my understanding to hold a vision of what else is possible for the world. I am aligned with values that reflect the preciousness of life, and I sustain a vision for a world that is aligned with heart. My steadfast commitment to my vision inspires others to join me in creating a world of equitable, sustainable peace.

EFT SETUP:

Even though things seem hard and challenging, I now choose to use my challenges to help me get clear about what I really want, and I deeply and completely love and accept myself.

EARTH:

Gate 39: Recalibration

Where do you need to tweak your perspective to see abundance where you think there is lack? How can you shift the story to see what you have versus what you think you don't? Spend some time practicing reframing your perspective this week.

JANUARY 6, 2024

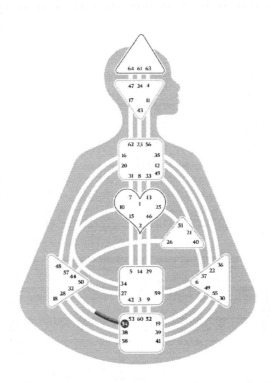

GATE 54: DIVINE INSPIRATION

CHALLENGE:

To learn to be a conduit for Divine Inspiration. To be patient and wait for alignment and right timing before taking action. To be at peace with stewardship for ideas and to learn to trust the Divine trajectory of an inspiration.

JOURNAL QUESTIONS:

What do I do to get inspired?

How do I interface with my creative muse?

Is there anything I need to do or prepare in order to be ready for the next step in the manifestation of my dream or inspiration?

How will I know when I am inspired? Will I feel it in my body?

AFFIRMATION:

I am a Divine Conduit for inspiration. Through me, new ideas about creating sustainability and peace on the planet are born. I tend to my inspirations, give them love and energy, and prepare the way for their manifestations in the material world.

EFT SETUP:

Even though I am afraid my dreams will not come true, I now choose to dream wildly and trust that my dreams will come true. All I have to do is focus my mind, trust, and know that all will unfold perfectly, and I deeply and completely love and accept myself.

EARTH:

Gate 53: Starting

What identities and attachments do you have about being the one who starts and finishes something? How can you deepen your trust in right timing?

JANUARY 11, 2024

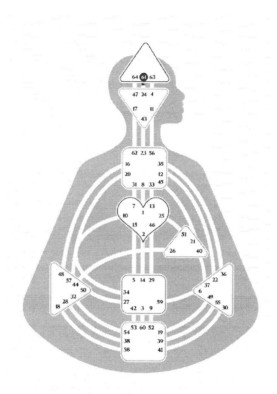

GATE 61: WONDER

CHALLENGE:

To not get lost in trying to answer or figure out why. To maintain a state of wonder. To not let the pressure of trying to know keep you from being present.

JOURNAL QUESTIONS:

What do I do to maintain my sense of wonder?

How can I deepen my awe of the magnificence of the Universe?

What old thoughts, patterns, and beliefs do I need to release in order to align with my knowingness and to trust my "delusional confidence" as a powerful creative state?

What greater perspectives on the events of my life can I see?

What are the greatest lessons I've learned from my pain?

How do I use these lessons to expand my self-expression?

AFFIRMATION:

I have a direct connection to a Cosmic perspective that gives me an expanded view of the meaning of the events in my life and the lives of others. I see the wonder and innocence of life and stay present in a constant state of awe. I am innocent and pure in my understanding of the world and my innocence is the source of my creative alignment.

EFT SETUP:

Even though I do not know all the answers, I now choose to surrender and trust that I am loved, supported, and nurtured by the Infinite Loving Source that is the Universe.

EARTH:

Gate 62: Preparation

This week's mantra: I am prepared. I'll know what I need to know when I need to know it. I know what to prepare when it's time to prepare it. I relax and trust in the flow. Repeat as needed.

JANUARY 11, 2024
NEW MOON

♑ Capricorn 20 degrees, 44 minutes
Gate 54: The Gate of Divine Inspiration

New Moon energy invites us to explore how we can deepen our alignment with our intentions and asks us to focus on what we want to grow and expand on in our lives.

The very first new moon of the calendar year and the last full moon of the Human Design year, initiates us by reminding us that we are vessels for the Cosmic Mind. The more connected with the Source through our practices and rituals, the more we are available to be inspired to create more in the world.

This new moon highlights our connection to our muse. It invites us to recommit to building a spiritual practice that, with consistent repetition, strengthens our connection to our creative inspiration. We are invited to spend some time with this moon connecting, reflecting, and allowing ourselves to become inspired.

These inspirations feed our dreams. It is not up to use to figure out how to make these inspirations come true. Our job is to listen, get inspired, and prepare the way. The more we prepare, the more we are positioned to receive. The more we receive, the more we can expand upon what we have. The more we expand upon what we have, the more we have to share.

We are being initiated and prepared to serve at our highest level.

CHALLENGE:

To learn to be a conduit for Divine Inspiration. To be patient and to wait for alignment and right timing before taking action. To be at peace with stewardship for ideas, and to learn to trust the Divine trajectory of an inspiration.

OPTIMAL EXPRESSION:

The ability to cultivate a deep relationship with the Divine Muse. To nurture the inspirational fruits of the muse, and to serve as a steward for an inspiration by aligning the idea energetically and preparing the way by laying foundational action and building.

UNBALANCED EXPRESSION:

To react to the pressure that you have to fulfill an inspiration and to use force to push the inspiration into form—even though it might not be your idea or dream to manifest, or the right time to bring it forth.

CONTEMPLATIONS:

What do I do to get inspired? How do I interface with my creative muse?

Is there anything I need to do or prepare in order to be ready for the next step in the manifestation of my dream or inspiration?

AFFIRMATION:

I am a Divine Conduit for inspiration. Through me, new ideas about creating sustainability and peace on the planet are born. I tend to my inspirations, give them love and energy and prepare the way for their manifestations in the material world.

JANUARY 17, 2024

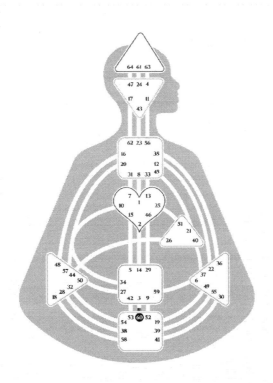

GATE 60: CONSERVATION

CHALLENGE:

To not let the fear of loss overwhelm your resourcefulness. To learn to find what is working and focus on it instead of looking at the loss and disruption.

JOURNAL QUESTIONS:

What change am I resisting?

What am I afraid of?

What are the things in my life that are working that I need to focus on?

Is my fear of loss holding me back?

AFFIRMATION:

I am grateful for all the transformations and changes in my life. I know that disruption is the catalyst for my growth. I am able to find the blessings of the past and incorporate them in my innovative vision for the future. I am optimistic about the future, and I transform the world by growing what works.

EFT SETUP:

Even though it is hard to let go of things that did not work, I now release all the clutter from the past, and I deeply and completely love, accept, and trust myself.

EARTH:

Gate 56: Expansion

Tell yourself a story about your life, your future and your dreams that causes you to expand energetically. Allow yourself to truly fill up your energy field with expansion.

SUMMARY

Your Quantum Human Design is your key to understanding your energy, your Life Purpose, your Life Path, and your Soul's Journey in this lifetime. You are a once-in-a-lifetime cosmic event and the fulfillment of your potential and purpose is the greatest gift you can give the world.

I hope this year has been revolutionary for you and that you re-connected with the true story of Who You Are and the power and possibility of your very special life.

If you need additional support and resources to help you on your Life Path and Soul's Journey, please visit the link below where you can find Specialists and Practitioners who will help you understand the story of your Human Design chart, coach you, and help you get to the root of any pain, blocks, or limiting beliefs that may be keeping you from enjoying your Life Story. There are all kinds of free goodies, videos, ebooks, and resources to help you on your way!

www.quantumalignmentsystem.com

Thank you again for being YOU! We are who we are because you are who you are!

From my heart to yours,
Karen

ABOUT THE AUTHOR

Karen Curry Parker is a Transformational Teacher, Speaker, and Coach. She is a multiple bestselling author, EFT (Emotional Freedom Techniques) Practitioner since 2000, Life Coach since 1998, original student of Ra Uru Hu, and one of the world's leading Human Design teachers since 1999. She is also a Quantum University PhD Student/Guest Lecturer and a TEDx Presenter.

Karen is the founder and creator of two certification trainings, the Quantum Human Design for Everyone Training System and The Quantum Alignment System and is also the founder of the Understanding Human Design Community. She is the host of the Quantum rEvolution and Cosmic Revolution Podcasts and co-founder of GracePoint Publishing.

Karen has a deep love for helping people activate their highest potential, which in part is why she created Quantum Human Design. Her core mission is to help people live the life they were designed to live by discovering who they are, what they are here to do, and how to activate their authentic Life Path by waking them up to the power of their innate creativity and unlimited possibility.

Karen is a 4/6 Time Bender (Manifesting Generator), mother of eight amazing humans, wife of a genius, and grandmother of two emerging world leaders. She has her BSN in nursing, BA in journalism, and is currently working on her PhD in integrative health at Quantum University.

RESOURCES

Enroll in courses
KarenCurryParker.Teachable.com

Join the community
KarenCurryParker.Circle.so

Want to become a Certified Quantum Human Design Specialist?
Enroll in Professional Training here:
QuantumAlignmentSystem.com/ProTraining

For more great books on Human Design, please visit our online store at
books.gracepointpublishing.com

If you enjoyed reading *2023 Quantum Human Design Evolution Guide* and purchased it through an online retailer, please return to the site and write a review to help others find this book.

Made in the USA
Las Vegas, NV
06 January 2023

65100717R00114